From There to Here
Journey
of a Skinned Rabbit

Sylvia Bryden-Stock

RCN, ONC, SCM, NDN Health Ed Cert
Reiki Master, Dip. Crystal Healing
Transformational Coach/Healer

BALBOA PRESS
A DIVISION OF HAY HOUSE

Copyright © 2013 Sylvia Elizabeth Bryden-Stock.

All rights reserved. No part of this book may be used or reproduced by any means, graphic, electronic, or mechanical, including photocopying, recording, taping or by any information storage retrieval system without the written permission of the publisher except in the case of brief quotations embodied in critical articles and reviews.

Balboa Press books may be ordered through booksellers or by contacting:

Balboa Press
A Division of Hay House
1663 Liberty Drive
Bloomington, IN 47403
www.balboapress.com
1 (877) 407-4847

Because of the dynamic nature of the Internet, any web addresses or links contained in this book may have changed since publication and may no longer be valid. The views expressed in this work are solely those of the author and do not necessarily reflect the views of the publisher, and the publisher hereby disclaims any responsibility for them.

The author of this book does not dispense medical advice or prescribe the use of any technique as a form of treatment for physical, emotional, or medical problems without the advice of a physician, either directly or indirectly. The intent of the author is only to offer information of a general nature to help you in your quest for emotional and spiritual well-being. In the event you use any of the information in this book for yourself, which is your constitutional right, the author and the publisher assume no responsibility for your actions.

Any people depicted in stock imagery provided by Thinkstock are models, and such images are being used for illustrative purposes only.
Certain stock imagery © Thinkstock.

Printed in the United States of America.

ISBN: 978-1-4525-8626-7 (sc)
ISBN: 978-1-4525-8627-4 (e)

Balboa Press rev. date: 11/11/2013

Acknowledgements

Thanks to my parents for their love and patience with my childhood health challenges and for doing the very best they could raising a family in the immediate post war years.

Blessings to all the people who have been a part of the rich tapestry of my life experiences. Without you I would not have grown and become the person I am today.

Special thanks to my dear friend Shirley, who diligently typed the script for this book and managed to read my typical "Nurse's scrawl". Also, for "being there" during some of the deepest challenges on my journey.

Thanks to my very special husband Brian, who has been supportive to me over the last sixteen years of our relationship as my Life Purpose finally evolved, without judgement or criticism and makes us laugh very single day in spite of the challenges we face.

Immense gratitude to my teachers and mentors who through seminars and training programmes helped me to finally, fully accept my true self and the purpose I am called to live out, to help humanity at this time of transformation on our beautiful Mother Earth.

Bob Proctor – Your Six Minutes to Success Programme gave me daily focus and incredible insights to pass on to others in my Life Purpose activities.

Wayne Dyer – for your great teachings and the privilege of seeing you live in London and feel the wonderful Universal Energy projected throughout the venue. Wayne you Inspire me!!

Christopher Howard – for your incredible Seminars here in London that facilitated some intense releasing of old patterns and courage to "just get on and do it!" The Wealth Propulsion Intensive" gave me great insight into the way forward with a Spiritual Calling through grounded Business Skills.

Les Brown – for your dynamic videos and books with a simple but powerful approach to living out ones purpose and staying motivated – Yes Les it is Possible!!!

Jack Canfield – for your Success Principles that gave me a structured approach to achieving Life Purpose Goals.

Dr Zi Ghang Sha for powerful healing modules and Karmic Release techniques.

Blessings and Love to my Spiritual Mastermind team with whom I daily communicate for inner guidance.

Thanks to a dear friend Polly Harper for kindly proof reading the text for me and constructive comments for a final "tweaking"

Thanks to Balboa Press for responding to publisher searches on the web when Sylvia had forgotten she had even contacted them!!!

Louise Hay – for your powerful book "You can Heal Your Life" which helped me to release old patterns and now is a valuable part of my Coaching and Healing Work Kit.

Foreward

It is my pleasure to share my story with you which was divinely guided in how and what has been written.

My intention with writing this book was to share with you the importance of allowing life to be our greatest teacher whilst benefitting our spiritual and soul development. I truly believe we are all part of that wonderful Creative Energy Force or "God" expressing through Human form here on earth. That being so, we may as well be the most amazing creator possible!

As I learned, it is never too late to realise "who we truly are" and live life from there knowing that subconsciously we have been anyway except maybe we didn't acknowledge it until now. The more we realise that all our experiences are just that, we can better understand why things occur and also take more conscious, divinely or soul guided choices and decisions in life that best serve us and promote ongoing amazing creations even if in the process, we make mistakes. All best creations go through testing times do they not?

Here you will read about my own twists and turns to discover her True Self and True Purpose.

May you laugh, learn and grow as you read on.

With blessings
Sylvia

Life is a Journey of Experiences

They Are Our Greatest Teacher

Learn Well and Have Fun as You dance Through Them

Contents

Part 1 – A Challenging Childhood with a Consistent Dream

Chapter 1	A Not So Grand Entrance!	1
Chapter 2	Early Memories	4
Chapter 3	"The Old Tin Hut and Much Much More!"	7
Chapter 4	School Plus Three Times on a Sunday	10
Chapter 5	At Last I Am "SAVED!"	16
Chapter 6	Lead Me Not into Temptation!	19
Chapter 7	Hormones, Strict Discipline & Routine	24
Chapter 8	Two Dogs, Two Budgerigars' and a Parrot	30
Chapter 9	Will I make my Dream Come True?	32

Part 2 – A Dream Comes True – Tales From the Nursing Years

Chapter 1	Was I prepared for the shock?	41
Chapter 2	No Excuses!	45
Chapter 3	The Grey Lady, A Cow and Sticky Floors	49
Chapter 4	Off with his leg! – GO!	54
Chapter 5	THE NEXT STEP: "Inmates" Over The Wall!	59
Chapter 6	Tears and Laughter	63
Chapter 7	The Goal Achieved!	69
Chapter 8	Thrown in the Deep End	74
Chapter 9	The Winding Road of Experience Begins	80
Chapter 10	Health – the Challenge re-emerges!	85
Chapter 11	Twists and Turns in my Nursing Career	89

Part 3 – Another Twist to The Journey

Chapter 1	A Leap of Faith!!	99
Chapter 2	In At The Deep End!	104
Chapter 3	The Camping Years	110
Chapter 4	Disillusionment – What is Next?	115
Chapter 5	Organised Chaos!	122
Chapter 6	It's Time To "Take Off"	125
Chapter 7	Yes – I Found My Soulmate!!	128
Chapter 8	Creating Balance is The Key	135

PART 1

A Challenging Childhood with a Consistent Dream

HMS SUSSEX

Chapter 1

A Not So Grand Entrance!

It is 1943 and Britain is still majorly at war. This year was an important one as it saw the support of the United States in our war against Hitler. Daddy was serving in the Royal Navy – he sneaked in at 16 yrs of age and after training in Portsmouth had a great career of 21 years with much of his time aboard HMS Sussex which was an active player in WWII.

I am the proud owner of his medals to this day and although he never spoke much about his naval years they were his favourite times. I would have loved to have heard some of the tales he would have had locked inside of him - happy times and others he encountered. I concluded he had some "great" times whilst based at Chatham in Kent for a time, whilst taking him for a memory trip to Chatham before he died. Living in that area at the time, Sylvia knew that it had been a typical Naval town with nearly every building yet another pub! He took great delight in pointing out the pubs still standing plus highlighting other sites as well as excitedly proclaiming "I remember good times in that pub!" Mummy being with us too, it was best not to let on what type of pubs they were as she would have been quite shocked! Suffice it to say he obviously had a "really great time" in the pubs!

Daddy never really made a great "land lubber" after leaving the Navy at the end of the war, changing jobs frequently within his qualifications as an Electrical Engineer. I do not think Mummy was happy for him to stay in the Navy although he reached the position of Chief Petty Officer. I believe Daddy would have captained his own ship if he could have continued his career. The pressure on Mummy as a naval officer's wife throughout the war years would have been extremely challenging. Having worked for a family "in service" prepared her for having to be very creative and frugal with food and general home management. This discipline continued throughout their married life together. She had amazing skill with meat carving – so thin to make it go round the family, you could almost see through it!

So here we are in July 1943 and Mummy must have conceived when Daddy was on leave 9 months previously. To be pregnant during those lean times in the UK was indeed a challenge with food scarcity and frequent air raids. Still, Mummy had been employed in service and was made of a strong constitution and even after the war was ended and rationing was still on she would make a meal out of "nothing"! The precision with which she was able to slice very thin bread as well as meat was amazing to watch. Forget about using a slicing machine – just call on Elsie Bryden if you want to stretch your resources!

I know that while she was carrying me, Mummy became very depressed and admitted to me in my adulthood that she actually was suicidal at one point. She conveyed this to me when I was going through my own personal crisis and having counselling and personal development training to eliminate old patterns and move forward. Knowing what we know now about the impact on the unborn child of feelings and emotions externally, it is no wonder that my growing physical body was impacted upon. More about that soon.

My birth came within the Cancerian Zodiac Sign which is one of the most sensitive signs of them all!

On 12th July I popped out at around 5.33 p.m. interrupting Mother's supper in the Hampton Wick Hospital. Apparently looking just like "A Skinned Rabbit", that was the beginning of an amazing journey with many twists and turns as my soul journeyed in this lifetime.

My one and only big Sister was 5 years old at this time and due to a very "Victorian" upbringing she was never told that I was "on the way". How she explained the bulging tummy of her mother I will never know unless, as we used to comment in my Midwifery training days, "she's carrying it all behind". It was many years later that I was to learn that Big Sister knew nothing of my pending arrival. That explained our rather "cool" relationship that existed over the decades. How important it is to communicate with children and help them accept realities rather than hide things from them. I believe they are more resilient than we give them credit for.

So on that fateful day Mummy goes into hospital and gives birth to another little baby girl who was not wanted during her pregnancy. Of course as my mother I am sure knew, once the baby is born it is a different story as the bonding begins. Two weeks later I am taken home and big sister is suddenly not "number one favourite" any more.

Thus began the saga of my life and sibling rivalry big time! The first six months of earthly life were not easy for Sylvia or the family as I cried most of the time with colic after my cows milk based feeds. For some reason, Mummy was not able to breast feed. I wonder how many bottles of good old fashioned gripe water were gone through! Never mind the sleepless nights! There was little knowledge of food intolerances at that time, otherwise my health journey might have been quite different!

As a young baby I knew nothing of the war going on but we were temporarily evacuated as were many children at the time. One vivid dream experience has stayed with me throughout the years. I was lying in my cot and suddenly the cot with Sylvia in it went tumbling down the stairs. Was I being picked up and rushed to a Shelter? Was my soul feeling the full impact of the physical body and falling to earth? Whatever the answer, it does not seem to have played a major role in my life experience for soul growth over the years.

Chapter 2

Early Memories

MANY PEOPLE HAVE vivid memories of their early years and some I have met can remember as far back as 9 months of age. As I recall early memories it is interesting that they are not joyous occasions but with my knowledge now it is clear that every moment was a.... choice – it took me years of experiencing and "life choices" to realise that all ones experiences are part of the journey we chose as a "soul" or "divine energy" spark prior to entering this world. No matter where our journey takes us, or the choices we make, we have the opportunity to learn and grow, impacting on our realisation of, and living in harmony with, who we truly are - Spirit incarnated through dense flesh to expand and become enlightened ready for the return to that other world from whence we came.

From the "colicky baby" I progressed to a toddler with frequent tummy upsets and eventually by the age of three or four I am sent by our General Practitioner to see a specialist. Of course back in the 1940's and 1950's little or nothing was known about lactose and wheat intolerance. Oh! If only the knowledge had been there! Although challenging, life would have been a great deal easier in terms of overall health.

With no car ownership at that time travel was solely by public transport. Off we went by bus – they pretty much always to time then - to the local hospital relying on the accuracy of the buses schedule as we would have had to change buses to get from Hayes to Hillingdon. I'm sure we arrived in plenty of time thanks to Mummy's good planning skills.

So there were Sylvia and Mother at the outpatient clinic nervously waiting for our turn. The consultant requests X-Rays and for a 3 year old this was a very daunting and terrifying experience. I vividly recall entering a very austere x-ray room and a tall figure in a white coat putting me on the X-ray table which seemed enormous as did the equipment being lowered down over my abdomen. I did as I was asked and kept very still – not too difficult wen filled with terror. Mummy did her best to re-assure me as I lay in dread of what might happen despite the explanations. I have great empathy for young children experiencing their first X-Ray or MRI Scan. Fortunately the X-ray would be read immediately with a return to the Consultant's Room. The words said to Mummy must have made her heart sink. I was not happy either as this was the beginning of a major guilt trip! "There is nothing wrong with her – tell her to chew her food properly!" came forth from the Doctor's mouth. The power of words! Especially in the years when as children we are a sponge soaking up information that creates our belief patterns!! The period up to and between five and seven years of age imprints dramatically on our subconscious and therefore will influence our core values and general self-esteem in later in life. Something worth thinking about if you are a parent or work with children.

Whether I did chew my food up to 32 times each mouthful remains to be seen – it did not have a major impact on my ensuing health issues. By now we are living in a house in West Ruislip, Daddy is out of the Navy and trying to adjust to being permanently on land. He kept rabbits as I recall to help with the meat intake for the family. Thankfully I did not witness their journey from hutch to cooking pot. Mummy's rabbit stew was delicious though! Add her scrumptious dumplings and, boy oh boy, a delicious meal! Pearl Barley was also part of the stew to help thicken and add nutrition. My interest also lay in working out the different bones and placing them together – infant pre-nursing training?? This caused great amusement around the meal table. Ok all you vegetarians reading this, times were hard at the end of the war and food was still scarce – at least the rabbits would have been humanely killed.

We had a pet dog – a white bull terrier cross called Creaser and when I sat on the kitchen table to be washed he laboriously licked the soap off which tickled and I would giggle uncontrollably and fidget making Mummy's task rather challenging. He looked cute in one of my dolls knitted bonnets and was always compliant if I wanted to open his mouth and count his teeth. He really was a softy and well trained by Daddy.

Living proof that, if a dog knows its place in the pack, it is not a problem and everyone is happy.

One Summer evening I was in bed – strict discipline on bedtime was part of the daily routine and there was no television to enlist a cry "Can't I watch the end of this?" The ice cream van would be heard playing its merry little tune outside my bedroom window as I tried to sleep whilst it was still daylight. Knowing I would probably be awake, Mummy appeared with a vanilla ice cream wafer on a saucer for me to eat. Indulgently I licked all round the sides of the wafer to soften the ice cream and then I sucked out the soft deliciously tasting ice cream until the wafer was soft and chewy. Oh what a delightful treat that was!!! Now I still drool over that indulgent experience because Dairy Ice Cream is a no-no on the food agenda since adulthood diagnosis of dairy and wheat intolerance.

Daddy was finding it difficult to stay in work after 21 years at sea and money was an issue at home. The house we lived in was on a mortgage and it was hard to maintain with Daddy's love of alcohol – ex naval officer? All part of the stress relieving strategy whilst at sea I suspect – got to be seen to be a team player! Add to that smoking strong and probably top price cigarettes along with Mummy smoking at that time. Finances were exceedingly tight.

I do remember that Mummy quit smoking when she "got saved" and church became her main focus. Smoking was considered to be the devils weed and a sin for those following their teachings. One way of promoting subtle health benefits I suppose before science kicked in its research evidence regarding smoking and health. Daddy never quit smoking but cut back dramatically on alcohol especially when he too "got saved" and involved in church matters in a big way.

Eventually due to financial pressures there was nothing to do but move to rented accommodation and that's when life took another turn....

Chapter 3

"The Old Tin Hut and Much Much More!"

It is January 1947 and it is a bitterly cold winter with a heavy fall of snow as the day dawns for our move to Hayes in Middlesex. What a time to be moving home! Stressful enough for Daddy and Mummy without the inclement weather! Eventually the removal van arrives at our new address of No. 52a Willow Tree Lane and unpacks all of our worldly goods.

Life was a bit crammed in an upstairs maisonette but with her great ability to "keep house", Mummy soon made it home. The family pewter tea set adorned the cupboard in the living room, pictures go up and homemade lace doilies adorned shelves and bedroom dressing tables. Somehow we all managed to eat around the kitchen table and foodstuff is stored in a typical kitchen cabinet with a drop down worktop. Even the old fashioned mangle is crammed in! The Belfast Sink in the corner caused many an argument over "washing up" duty which was delegated to big sister and I. Of course, being five years my senior and jealous of my ever appearing on Mother Earth, big sister always chose the better of the two according to her mood – washing or drying the dishes. "Stop your arguing and get on with it!" Mummy would say firmly – "Yes but she always gets to......." I would retort but somehow Sister got the better of me every time.

How Mummy coped in the small kitchen I never knew. Washing was either, soaked in the bath, or done in the sink and mangled through the green coloured free standing "thing" with rollers and a handle to turn them. The sheets and any flat articles were fed through the rollers as the other hand turned the handle so that the rollers squeezed out the water which collected in a bucket beneath. The washing was then hung out on the line in our small garden to dry. Sheets and Whites were done in the old fashioned copper which was filled with hot water and almost boiled the cotton items to get them whiter than white.

The Launderette came to the rescue sometimes until a small washing machine was purchased plus an accompanying spin dryer. A lovely blue whitener tablet known as Dolly Blue was added to the "Whites" wash to make them really bright. Mummy took great pride in her washing and ironing – not a crease to be seen in anything. Obviously high standards were brought with her from her time in service. Robin Starch Powder was always present in the house and lovingly she starched pillow cases, tablecloths, sheets and of course Daddy's shirt collars – he wore shirts of the time, that had separate collars.

Being married to an ex Naval Officer meant that everything had to be "in order". Not just the clothing items but the home as well. Daily polishing and wielding of the vacuum cleaner with the sturdy Electrolux cylinder vacuum cleaner was never to be forgotten except of course on Sundays when, after a "Spiritual Conversation" Sundays were sacrosanct for worship only – God's day of "rest" became our day of "rest" – more about that to come!

Not long after we moved to Hayes we became friends with the next door but one neighbour who were regular attendees of the local "Apostolic" Pentecostal Church down the road. A rather unusual building of not extensive proportions it had a corrugated tin roof and was affectingly known as "The Old Tin Hut". That Old Tin Hut was to change my life forever.

Winter at "52a" was literally a "bitter" experience. We had no central heating – just an open coal fire in the living room. We dreaded going to the cold bathroom and getting undressed for bed was not any more pleasant. Winter bedtime was flannelette pyjamas, thick socks and into bed with a stone hot water bottle at my feet. Eventually one warmed up – head under covers except nostrils peeping out to breathe in the ice cold air. Morning was greeted by scraping ice from the **inside** of the window. Some still argue that single glazing is healthier as often with double glazing some folks refrain from opening windows AT all during the winter. This breathing stale air all the time – is a great recipe for lethargy and "tiredness". Toasting crumpets and roasting chestnuts was a joyous pastime with the open fire – until a gas fire was installed so that humping buckets of coal upstairs from the bunker outside no longer took place. No more roasted chestnuts or toasted crumpets. Crumpets grilled never tasted the same somehow.

Mummy became close friends with our next door but one neighbour and one day was invited to "The Old Tin Hut" for a "Women's Meeting". I think she found a degree of solace there as there were still struggles at home with Daddy "Job Hopping" as well as drinking and smoking. Often I would hear rows as I tried to sleep at night which upset the sensitive Cancerian child and throughout life I would not enjoy hearing voices raised in argument around me. Butterfly feelings in my Solar Plexus were regular occurrences especially around arguments or someone shouting at another person before I began my journey of release to empowerment.

So Mummy began to attend "The Old Tin Hut" more regularly and one day announced her "conversion" experience and that she now had Jesus in her heart and inner peace and joy. She gave up smoking and any alcohol that she may have enjoyed – in moderation compared to Daddy. Big Sister recalls Mummy giving an ultimatum "It's either Me or the Drink!!" She Won!!!

Daddy seemed little interested in attending the church as although he grew up in Dublin where Catholicism would have been the main religion he became an Agnostic during his youth with no firm belief in God.

However, events were about to change all that……………!

Chapter 4

School Plus Three Times on a Sunday

July 1947 was the year I became eligible to start attending school and I was soon the proud possessor of the local primary school uniform – Yeading Primary School was a fair walk away for a five year old but walk we did – no car to jump in. Just wrap up warm on cold winter days and briskly walk to keep warm.

Still having problems with my gut system and the beginning of frequent throat and ear infections began an interesting journey through Infant and Junior School Years. Part of the daily ritual was to have one of Daddy's beautifully ironed ex Naval Khaki hankies with me when I went to school. This was in case anyone bumped into me and knocked my nose causing it to bleed. That happened fairly regularly unfortunately.

By now at five years of age I had a dream of becoming a nurse – just like Daddy's Grandmother. Always looking pale and ill you can imagine the comments of adults around me – "She wants to be a nurse? Can't see that happening with her poor health. She's always having to miss school!" How easy it would be to listen to those words and truly believe them. Somehow an inner determination took over and I did not let my dream die.

It is so important to hang onto our dreams and believe in them – they just might become reality!

Everything seemed against me – Infection after infection plus more nosebleeds and one fateful night I called Mummy as my nose started to bleed again. This time it would not stop and the doctor had to pack my nose to get it to stop. I was a brave girl and a few days later when Daddy drew the short straw to gently remove the pack, thankfully all was well. As that was not enough many nights were spent asking Mummy to pray to God to take away the pain in my left ear as once more infection had set in with a burst ear drum making me almost deaf in my left ear – I was in trouble for keep on saying "pardon?" repeatedly or "not listening". Truth was I could not hear properly. However my right ear compensated well and I began to top up with unconscious lip reading. There is always a way round challenges and children seem better at finding it than adults as they are less "programmed".

At around the age of nine years, part of school routine was to attend swimming lessons at a local swimming baths. Bravely I went along with the class and donned my typical school swimsuit which was far from elegant, especially on a skinny pale looking little girl! *Not much different to how mummy described me at birth in later years – "you looked just like a Skinned Rabbit when you were born!"* Sadly that was my first and last lesson as Mummy was told by our General practitioner that I was not to get water in my ear due many burst ear drums. Oops!! Another programming, for fear of later learning to swim in a swimming pool! No problem floating in the sea in later life in spite of no "sides" to hold on to when practicing. Mummy reckoned she could teach me to swim but she was also banned from swimming following a kidney infection. So Sylvia is one of the many adults still unable to swim but not afraid to go into a swimming pool and try, plus loves to go in the sea – preferably in warmer climes than the UK.

School was not my most favourite time as I was really shy and withdrawn in my own world, having only a few friends and now being taken regularly to the Old Tin Hut after Mummy's conversion experience.

I would spend a lot of time staring out of the living room window just "being" and daydreaming. One day as I was staring out of the window I stopped and called Mummy. "Mummy, Mummy quickly – look it is raining on the other side of the road and this side of the road it isn't!" "You are right" commented Mummy "that can happen if there are not enough rain clouds to make it rain on both sides of the road. The wonders of nature in full view.

Despite a great deal of time absent from school I did well and was good at spelling and mental arithmetic because I could visualise the letters and numbers in my mind. Embroidery and sewing were of great interest to me and as well as school lessons Mummy was a great teacher. I recall embroidering a simple tray cloth at barely five years of age and I still have in my possession a needle holder I made aged 9 years.

Weekends were also a bit of a ritual and my Sister and I were expected to do chores and shopping to help us learn basic life skills. The local shops supplied vegetables and other basic ingredients – the grocery store had special wooden "butter" pats and a wooden board to make a block of butter for you after extracting a lump of butter from a large block that had been delivered. Pre-packed had not yet come about. Remember, this was the early 1950's and Britain was still recovering from the war and rationing still in place through many of the 1950's decade. Watching the assistant creating decorative butter blocks fascinated me. Never mind the Greaseproof paper cones by creating a cone shape and twisting the bottom so that sugar could be poured in after being weighed on good old fashioned scales with varying weights from ounces to pounds. Biscuits came in large boxes and were weighed. Broken ones were sold for a lot less and helped the finances stretch further. Recently I actually saw in a supermarket (2012) a pack of broken biscuits for sale in a very colourful wrapping!

Of course we never missed a bath and hair washing on a Friday evening. As I said earlier, Mummy would say "come on Friday Night's Amami Night" The word "Amami" comes from a brand of shampoo that mummy would have used.

With long hair for most of my childhood and teens I did not relish this at all. Brushing long hair by Mummy was a very painful experience followed by enduring the tight plaits.

Around the age of ten years old, I had my hair cut somewhat shorter and then more suffering ensued for a little girl with very straight hair. Ringlets were fashionable for girls at that time and I was not to be left out! Every night there was a pre-bedtime ritual when Mummy gathered long pieces of cotton rags torn from an old sheet and methodically proceeded to part my hair into sections taking a section at a time and, winding tightly round the hair from bottom to the head created false twirls all over my head. "Ouch" I would cry as the hair got more and more pulled. "Stand still" would be the retort! So with gritted teeth I did as I was told. This agony was followed by having to sleep in them until morning. Then began another torture as the rags were removed, and, as if by magic, I had a head of ringlets that, somehow, stayed in place for most of the day. This experience would be matched only by the use of spiky hair rollers in my nursing days which I slept in to create a good hairstyle the following day. What we do for our vanity!! Thank goodness for the "Cut & Blow Dry" era that developed with creative styles minus the agony!

By Friday evening the weeks washing was complete and adorning the wooden airer overhead in the kitchen – not a crease to be seen in any vest or knickers and whiter than white.

Sunday morning began the "day of rest" with kippers for breakfast – Daddy's favourite. I liked them too but did not enjoy pulling on clean underwear afterwards that reeked of kippers. I have often wondered if we stank the church out with our super clean clothes perfumed with eau-de-kippers!

Off to the Old Tin Hut by 11.00 a.m. for morning service - without Daddy to begin with. I loved the hymn singing, accompanied by the lady organist who pumped away with her feet to keep it churning out the tunes for us - she always sat upright exceedingly proud of her "Calling" to play for us. There was a reading from the Bible and prayers – not structured prayers like the Church of England or Catholics but impromptu praying – anyone could stand up and say a prayer asking God to forgive us for not living out the message of salvation enough plus healing prayers for the sick. Sometimes there were "outpourings of the Holy Spirit" – where members of the congregation spoke strange words that were said to be like when the disciples received the "the gift of Tongues" as written in the book of Acts in the Bible. Strange at first I soon became "ok" with this. Before we all took bread and wine to celebrate communion with Christ there would be a sermon from the Pastor – usually the message was to encourage us to be more "faithful to the Lord" and not let sin take us away from our path. Sin was things like smoking and drinking, going to the pictures or theatre – in fact anything that might keep you away from "The Lord's House" which in our case was the Old Tin Hut. We always wore our Sunday Best (over the kipper perfumed underwear) and a hat had to adorn all the ladies heads. "Women must keep their heads covered" would be quoted from the New Testament.

Where other families were off out at Bank Holiday weekends we trundled to various other Apostolic Churches for the "Weekend Convention" – all day Saturday and Evening worship plus Sunday and Monday. Definitely no time to sin!!!! In spite of the incredible control and feeling of guilt if I hadn't got anything to say sorry to God for. I still value the power present in the churches and witnessed some remarkable healing of people and also entity releases and of course not forgetting the hearty singing and clapping. No chance of feeling sad when the singing began. There is nothing quite like a good sing to lift the spirit within. It is excellent therapy if one is going through challenging times and I still love a good sing! Easter weekend convention would see ladies adorned with a new suit and hat. There was a sort of competitive spirit with who looked the best and the men would graciously give positive comments which was a great ego boost! We always hoped for good weather so that a light weight almost summer style suit could be paraded around. There was disappointment if the carefully chosen outfit had to stay in the wardrobe until the Whitsun Convention!

After Mummy's conversion experience Daddy slowly became interested and was to have his own conversion experience which did help giving up alcohol. Not so sure about the smoking though. I cannot recall seeing him without cigarettes. He migrated from strong Naval Cigarettes to Old Holborn Tobacco and would roll his own with great dexterity and precision. I have to thank Daddy for his helping Sylvia in not wanting to smoke. It was not the fact that it was a "sin" to indulge in "the weed" that prevented me ever wanting to smoke. It was, when aged about 10 years I saw one of his butt ends in an ashtray and thought to myself "If Daddy enjoys this it must be nice!!!" I then proceeded to pick up the cigarette end and put it to my mouth to chew. As soon as my teeth and tongue touched it the absolute repulsive taste hit me – that was enough! Never was a cigarette ever going to be on the agenda in my life!

Daddy became an active member of the Church and was one of the main preachers at ours and other churches. I was always proud of him and how he would speak according to his own interpretation of the scripture which might challenge some. He would also read and study other teachings and philosophies. He left the Apostolic Church after a time and became a local preacher with the Methodist Church. I would often travel with him on his preaching itineraries – these were some of my favourite times.

Eventually Daddy stopped going to the churches as he became more disillusioned with the "dogma" as he would call it. Before he passed over, when asked what he would spiritually call himself he stated "I suppose I would call myself a Christian Communist!" Well!!! Work that one out if you can!

When Sylvia reflects on her life with all it's twists and turns there is a very strong resemblance to Daddy and the way he progressed with his spirituality. Like him Sylvia was pleased to be released from total "religious control" to a "free thinking" person literally "working out her own salvation" as is quoted in the Bible in the book of Philippians chapter 2 verse *12 "Wherefore, my beloved, as ye have always obeyed, not as in my presence only, but now much more in my absence, work out your own salvation with fear and trembling"*

This may sound a little irreverent, but Sylvia, over the years, has certainly worked out her own salvation with much fear and trembling!

Chapter 5

At Last I Am "SAVED!"

Everything had it's purpose and it was considered right and proper to dress well and look good – the dreaded ringlets when going to God's House. A new outfit would be the thing for the Easter Convention – usually a lightweight almost Summer outfit which was great if the weather was warm. Much discussion went on about who was wearing what and it was a bit like Hollywood or the Baftas – I am sure there was a little bit of competition to be the best dressed lady of the weekend. New hats adorned too, just as they do on Lady's Day at the famous Ascot Races. No harm done! I am sure that God did not mind a little rivalry or what we were wearing at all!.

Without realising it at the time I was already "seeing things" which would years later develop into "Spiritual Insight" skills and channelling messages of comfort and guidance from loved ones guides in God's Spirit World. During most events I would see either a white or gold aura around the minister or Pastor as they were called and many of the visiting Speakers. I would also see a light in the form of a person but without full physical manifestation standing just behind whoever was preaching. It was all quite natural to me and I never spoke of it to anyone. In prayer I would be bathed in light and feel heat in my body and arms. Later I would become a Reiki Healer and Teacher.

Sometimes I would see shapes of people like the old greyish photograph negatives on walls in friends' houses. Again I said nothing as it seemed normal to me.

At Last I Am "SAVED!"

1953 was an important year. Yes, it was the Queen's Coronation and we had a street party which was great fun. Flags and and lots of food and general merriment. It was also the year when Billy Graham was holding a rally at the Haringey Arena. Although regularly attending church, I had never heeded to the call to be "saved and give my heart to Jesus" by going down to the front for prayers to be said at the end of the Preacher's sermon – they kept on asking till someone eventually conceded.

At Major Conventions some people would repeat their "getting saved" call which I found a little odd. If you already had Jesus in your heart why did you have to keep asking him in? Anyway, off we trotted to Haringey and are sitting high up near the back of the arena. Lots of singing, praying and the then famous Beverley Shea Spiritual Singer sang a couple of hymns followed by Billy Graham's preaching. He was dynamic and something stirred within me. At the call to accept Jesus a stirring in my solar Plexus made me go all the way down to the front of the arena with many, many others and I accepted Jesus into my life.

Little did I realise then that as my life panned out I would work with his power in a very different way as will be revealed in subsequent chapters. There was much rejoicing by church members because Sylvia had at last had her sins forgiven and would be eligible to enter heaven – so long as she never "walked away from Jesus" as they taught steps fear!" Now I am saved and I must obey the rules. This created challenges with certain school curricular. Going to the pictures was a sin and Sylvia was already so programmed, that fear of any "no's" made asking for things a terrifying, gut twisting experience.

Remember 1953 that Queen Elizabeth II was crowned? – a film of this was to be shown at the local cinema and a school trip organised. It is part of the education you see - so how do I ask if I can go? After all I will be committing a sin, yet I desperately wanted to go. Somehow the courage, mixed with butterflies in my belly as big as elephants arises and I ask if I can go. Much discussion about it ensues between Mummy and Daddy and the educational argument wins the day. Phew!!! Thank goodness; as to tell my friends I was not going would have been as big a challenge.

The day dawns for the trip and Sylvia joins her classmates as they board the hired coach that will take them to the closest cinemas showing the crowning of our queen. There was a sense of added excitement to be partly "sinning" and being able to "get away with it". On arrival we followed teachers and usherettes to take our allotted seats. To my friends this was a common occurrence and just another fllm that had extra excitement to it. Sylvia indulged herself in the whole agenda of the day just wishing this could be a more frequent part of life.

I thoroughly enjoyed seeing a full colour presentation of the coronation and excitedly reported the whole trip to Mummy and Daddy later. Whether they showed enthusiasm or a passing acknowledgement due to the teachings at The Old Tin Hut has faded from memory but Sylvia sure did enjoy the change from the life of strict control. Here was fun and happiness in life's day to day happenings.

We have to face fear and risks no's. How incredible that such fear could grip hold when one is taught from the Bible "Ask and It shall be given you, seek and ye shall find, knock and the door will open"!!

Eventually – many years later for Sylvia – she learned to overcome the fear and asked for things anyway. A no would ultimately lead to the very best "yes" situation.

Chapter 6

Lead Me Not into Temptation!

Following my conversion I became a dedicated member of the Apostolic faith and was ready to "convert" the world. I did my best to live it out at school; but felt isolated and desperately desired to be part of the crowd. Shyness continued as did my health challenges but deep down my dream of having a successful nursing career was firmly fixed. Daddy was pleased with this as his hopes were that I would achieve my dream and become a Matron like his Grandmother.

As I said previously, School was not my favourite pastime so memories are few. I do recall struggling with some of the maths and although I possessed a creative mind the typical problem solving maths always got low marks as did a typical intelligence test at the age of ten years prior to sitting the "Eleven Plus" exam for a place in Grammar School – preferable for a Nursing Career.

Big Sister was already studying at the local Grammar School and doing quite well but with no strong career goals. She ended up working as a Secretary Clerk at the Prudential Insurance Company and not going to University - much to Mummy and Daddy's disappointment. They felt that she wasted her Grammar School Education.

I tried desperately to make up for any lost school days and was eligible to take the Eleven Plus exam for a Grammar School Place. Oh the disappointment when I failed by only a couple of marks and had to go to the local secondary school. My inadequacy rose and it showed itself in sports and team events. Somehow I always seem to end up on the losing side – the red team! Being very sensitive I would get quite upset at losing – life seemed to be against me all the time!.

I could easily have given up on my dream but it would not leave me. Back then it was possible to sit another exam at the age of thirteen and get a place at Technical College. Once again I was chosen as a candidate for this exam and passed with good marks for a place at Chiswick Polytechnic as it was known as then. Although overjoyed, I am sure Mummy and Daddy also had pangs of worry about having to pay for my uniform plus the fares to and from college each day involving bus and train fares. Somehow it all came together and off I went to continue my journey through the growing up years. I was registered to study Domestic Science and then move on to a Pre-Nursing course. Already I was beginning to see the way towards my dream.

Church was still the number one focus and a major "peer group" challenge at college. What had I to talk about? We only went to Sunday and weekday meetings at the Old Tin Hut and listen to a little radio. Even Television which was becoming more popular was another "thing of the devil". Still, we did have Jesus at home and indulged playing card games – no money involved of course! Gambling was big on the list of sins as well. Dominoes were fun and I loved doing Jigsaw puzzles. When the weather was fine we would play in the orchard with our neighbours' children. They had a son and two daughters. Big Sister eventually ended up marrying the elder son – a good solid "Apostolic" marriage with brother in law a regular Preacher and Sister a solo singer in some of the services complete with the statutory adornment of her hat that actually did not cover the head as quoted in the scriptures. More like a pimple on an elephant!!! Never Mind – she was wearing a hat I suppose.

By the age of 12 years it was expected that all services were attended Sunday morning, Sunday School, Evening Service plus the Prayer Meeting and Bible Study night during the week. There was no respite, not even with all the homework. Many a week I would have the same command ringing in my ears "Hurry up and get your homework done it's Prayer Meeting night"! There were times when homework seemed a much sweeter choice than prayer meetings. There were my school pals out with friends, allowed to go to the pictures and generally have fun while my life revolved around wearing out my knees and singing Halleluiah – never mind "invite" us

Lead Me Not into Temptation!

to come and get saved!!! In spite of wishing I could be like my friends. I was a dutiful Servant of the Lord and keen to help others get saved from the wrath of Hell Fire. You see, no matter how loving and giving one was and leading a life of great service to mankind, if you had not asked Jesus to forgive your sins on bended knee and ask him into your heart you were destined to live an afterlife of burning hell! How strange when God is so loving! God and Jesus taught love as the key to all things along with taking responsibility for one's life. "Religiousl Indigestion" was almost set in whilst college was a great respite from this and gave me a taste of what life was really like.

On some days at lunchtimes I would walk to Chiswick High Road with my best mate to an Italian Cafe and get a free lunch as we looked after the ladies little ones for an hour to give her a break. Of course Mummy and Daddy did not know – a punishment would have been handed out big time. Just like when I was at Secondary School enjoying being in the Country Dance Team with my partner who became my first "infatuation" or as I thought he was my true love. We would not buy dinner ticket and sneak to the chip shop at the top of Willow Tree Lane – we lived at No. 52A, and buy some chips. Not a wise venue as one day Mummy saw us and marched me home. Her tongue was worse than if she had given me a beating. "You will now come here for lunch everyday" How dare you be behaving like that with this boy" I was broken hearted, the world had come to an end and I sobbed in bed for many a night but eventually got over it. Not only was I seeing a boy - he wasn't saved with Jesus in his heart. I yielded and had to say sorry to God!

Having come to terms with "lost love" I am really delighted when a school trip of a week to the Isle of Wight was on offer. I hoped and prayed I would be able to go – luckily Mummy and Daddy agreed that the air would also do me good and somehow got the money together. I am both excited but nervous of being away from my comfort zone and weekly rigid routine. The excitement somehow seemed to override the fear. Mummy packed my case in her usual "perfect" way with all the required clothes and finding the allowed spending money.

Off we go – coach and ferry and end up at a large guesthouse in Shanklin. We shared rooms and all of us had a few extras of sweets and biscuits in our cases. Typically we decided one night to have a midnight feast and arranged to meet in one of the girls' rooms. Somehow it did not happen – a few of us slept through the night. Trips were organised to see the thatched cottages and shops and St. Catherine's Lighthouse is a must.

Oh my! Here comes a massive challenge. Sylvia does not do heights and here we are at the lighthouse and destined for the top to see the light reflectors and admire the view. My heart is racing; I am all in a panic and need encouraging up the spiral staircase – "Don't look down!" I say to myself and immediately my eyes disobey the mental command. Sick feelings engulf my stomach and now fear kicks in. I make it to the top of the spiral staircase, breathe a sigh of relief only to notice another straight metal ladder against the wall that leads to the lights and viewing platform. I bravely climb up making sure someone is in front of me and behind me, desperately trying to hide my overriding fear and panic. Heartbeat settles a bit and I courageously look out to sea whilst the lighthouse keeper chats on. Just as I am becoming a little calmer it is announced that it is time to return to the bottom. This seems to be an even worse torture to Sylvia but she cannot stay where she is so with baited breath and a stomach in huge knots of panic I descend, trying desperately hard not to look over the side of the staircase. At last! Safely down – I never went up a lighthouse again in spite of going through my fear but have become better at dealing with heights.

At home I was prone to let things slip through my fingers to the floor – sometimes crockery. Daddy used to call me "butterfingers" because butter is slippery and nothing would stick to it. Well, I lived up to "butterfingers" 100% when we visited Alum Bay to collect various coloured sands. My personally filled glass tube would be a present for Mummy and Daddy on return home. It's a long trudge down to the beach – since then a chair lift has been erected – but I would rather walk down. We are all kitted out with a spoon and test tube tightly gripped in our hands ready to collect the coloured sand – there are many different colours due to the way sedimentation took place over millions of years. Enthusiastically, everyone fills their test tube including me. As I stood up and started upward I tripped. Up in the air went the test tube and spoon and as the filled tube of many colours hit the ground it smashed! I was mortified and so upset that my gift so carefully gathered was now reduced to smithereens. Reluctantly I purchased a tube of coloured sand to take home but it was not the same as the one I had lovingly filled. Mummy graciously and lovingly accepted it when I got home. The rest of the trip went smoothly as we toured the island and then it was homeward bound with an essay to write. That was not such a great idea for us especially as marks would be given for the assignment. But then life is a mixture of perceived "nice" and not so "nice" experiences isn't it? The "not so nice" helps us appreciate more the "nice" things. Of course ultimately it is all "experience" and helps the "inner self" or "soul" with it's progression whilst journeying through physical form here on Mother Earth, as Sylvia was to realise years later as she spirituality expressed itself in very different ways to how she was programmed during childhood.

Chapter 7

Hormones, Strict Discipline & Routine

At the age of 12 Sylvia still had no idea how babies were born. I knew they grew in a woman's tummy but how they came out I did not have a clue. Maybe the fairies magiced them through the belly button?

We never saw Mummy and Daddy naked let alone in a warm embrace and kissing. Biology lessons at college were very useful in explaining the more "intimate" details of conception and birth, learning firstly about amoeba. Not that stretching a poor worm onto a board to examine it was of great help! Dissecting a dead frog was not exactly inspiring either! The smell of formaldehyde in which dead animals and fish are kept made one feel quite nauseous.

The biology teacher always extracted them from the stinking liquid with great joy and pride laying them on the biology laboratory slab with determination to teach us how cells are formed and what the guts of a fish or frog looked like. Learning about plant photosynthesis was much less traumatic.

Amazing that I still wanted to be a nurse, which would involve all sorts of human horrors to be met along the way.

Suddenly the teen hormones began to kick in and Mummy decided that it was time to "tell me a few things". The day still stays vividly in my memory even now. I had just returned home from school and Mummy let me get settled in; then grabbing her knitting called me to the kitchen. She sat in a chair facing me - what have I done now? I thought must be in trouble again! (taking the blame for a jealous big sister gave me many a slap on the legs over the years). "Sit Down. Sylvia, I need to talk to you" click clack go the knitting needles - knit one, pearl one etc. She was obviously embarrassed but took a deep breath and began to explain how girls grow breasts and also have "periods" "Periods?" "Whatever are these? I thought instantly. The word period was associated with time lapses in English language and grammar! "You will have a period (that word again) every month and bleed from down below" Where exactly "down below" was the next mental question. "It will come suddenly so you must be prepared wherever you go!" When you have periods it means you can get pregnant - another new word - so you must keep away from boys!!! Well!!! Was I confused or what...? Mummy gives a sigh of relief that sex education is done and proceeds to put down her knitting and put the kettle on the gas hob to make a pot of tea.

5 p.m. was the tea time ritual. The "In Service" and Naval routines meant that we had strict meal times. Sunday was different due to God's day of rest routine which was always roast dinner, cooked on a low oven heat while we praised God and took communion in the old Tin Hut.

Tea time was immaculately cut bread and butter slices – Mummy could make a loaf of bread go a long way. Sometimes slices were so thin you could almost see through them. We either had homemade jam sandwiches or sometimes paste – my favourite was sardine and tomato - followed by homemade fruit cake or Victoria Sponge and sometimes homemade Jam tarts. Yummy!!

Mummy was a superb cook and could stretch the Sunday roast meat for another two days at least. Typically our weekly menu was:-

Roast on Sunday, Cold on Monday, Minced on Tuesday, Wednesday Pie or Stew, Thursday Liver and bacon or similar, Fish on Friday – no catholic influence or Pentecostal stipulations - and Sausages on Saturday.

Nothing was wasted, bones were made into stock and every morsel of dinner had to be eaten to get your dessert. These were typical home made of that era – Baked Rice Pudding with Jam, Steamed Sultana Pudding, Stewed Fruit, Baked Sponge with a Jam base. All were served with either Birds or Brown & Polsons Custard made reasonably "runny" to make it go a long way.

Whilst big sister, Mummy and myself indulged in sandwiches and cake Daddy's dinner which was prepared at lunchtime would be warming over a simmering pan of hot water and ritually served him after his "welcome home" cup of tea on arrival home from work with slippers waiting for hm.

Apart from my "liaison" with the country dance partner there was little chance of "yielding to temptation" as the first two years at college was all girls. This "liaison" was during the lunch hour, when we would sneak to the local chip shop together. Stupidly we were visiting the one very close to home and one fateful day – yes you have guessed - Mummy was going to the shops and spied us together. "You get back home my girl!" she cried. Sheepishly I waked the short distance home with her and got the telling off of my life about deceit, and from that day forth until I moved on to Chiswick College lunches were at home and I was not to see him again. You can imagine how heartbroken I was, crying every night in bed feeling bereft of my first love!

Very soon after that I was to pass the 13 plus exam and go to Chiswick College where preparations towards gaining a nursing career would begin. This would incur further challenges to the home budget as there was a strict uniform code and Mummy had spent precious income on heavy pale green linen dresses for me. Imagine how Sylvia felt when she arrived at college for the first summer term to see all her friends in lovely pale green and white striped dresses with trendy short puffed sleeves and gathered skirts. On dear! Sylvia was SO out of place and on top of the shyness due to the restricted childhood her Self Esteem rocketed downwards. There was only one thing to do – drip on to Mummy for new dresses! And thus I did! When I look back at this scenario I feel for her as, there was Sylvia desperate to be "part of the group" and conform for inner comfort, with Mummy thinking of the further strain on the home budget. After all big sister went to grammar school and goodness knows what expense was incurred for that! Well – surprise, surprise –Mummy must have felt sorry for me because I got my own way in the end.

Another scenario was not as so successful. Time to replace my shoes that were very careworn. A trip to Hounslow High Street was planned - there were at least twelve shoe shops adorning the high street to choose from. Starting at one end and working our way down, I began again trying to get what I wanted. This was the time of heeled shoes with pointed toes and the girls in my class were all coming to college in varying heights and slimness of heels along with toes crammed into very tight pointed toe styles!

"I want to try those on – all the girls are wearing those shoes now!" I longingly bleated to mummy. "No!" was the stern reply as she asked the assistant to bring out heavy looking "sturdy" black slip-on shoes for me to try on. Near to tears Sylvia pleaded with her to no avail." It's this pair or the others – **or** – you wear what you are wearing even if they get holes in the bottom!" Very reluctantly I gave in as I knew that I was on a losing battle. Reflecting on that time, plus the nurse training shoe regulations, I can honestly say that my feet have maintained good shape with straight toes unlike many girls of the time (and boys) who ended up in hospital having surgery to straighten toes that were totally misshapen due to the wearing of the wrong shoes. The things we do for vanity. Well! Thank you Mummy for getting me off to a good "footing" in life!!

It's ironic how we don't appreciate things that happen in life until maybe years later when we see the benefits of a perceived very difficult experience. That does not necessarily have to be childhood experiences either.

The first two years before I commenced the official Pre-nursing Course was "all girls" with hormones starting to kick in. Moods swings were rife due to the varying monthly cycles – a nightmare for the teachers. I soon settled in and had a lovely bunch of new friends. Discussions around weekend activities brought the "tummy butterflies" syndrome regularly as I could only talk of yet another "churchy" thing which was boring to most of the girls. Even worse was when it was Bank Holidays and School holidays! "what did you do?" they would ask with excitement and bated breath. "Oh My!" What do I say? It has been yet another church convention or trip to an annual major gathering in Penygroes in Wales where visiting Pastors came and laboured forth with challenging sermons and we all re-confirmed our commitment to our faith".

Sylvia tried her very best to focus on the activities that took place in between the services so that it sounded like a great fun activity holiday. "Witnessing for Christ" was not easy for a shy teenager who desperately wanted to bond with the group. It was to be years later that Sylvia realised that it is perfectly OK to speak out and not be ashamed of what one stands for.

It is SO important that we develop our own inner values and live by them, respecting others life values but not compromising our own values and beliefs, just to be liked.

I enjoyed the cookery classes which began with the first lesson on how to thoroughly clean ones fingernails and push back the cuticles so that every half moon at the nail base showed. Inspections took place and "Miss" always knew if your nails had not been attended to daily.

Typically we cooked various foods – savoury and sweet - which were proudly presented at home to long suffering parents who graciously praised the attempt to create great cuisine. I never could match Mummy's cooking of course.

There was one fateful cookery lesson I shall never ever forget! We all had various ingredients cooking away on our gas cookers. I was boiling potatoes as I recall. Typically with "Miss" out of our eye shot we were being silly and generally messing around. Suddenly there is an intensive smell of burning from somewhere in the classroom – Oh my! It's coming from the direction of Sylvia's cooker. With baited breath I approached cautiously and lifted the lid of my supposedly boiling potatoes – Horror of Horrors!! – the pan had boiled dry!! Even worse there were large flames coming up through the bottom of the saucepan!! I quickly put the lid back on and turned off the gas. Fear gripped me in my gut. How do I explain to "Miss", let alone Mummy and Daddy who probably would have to pay for a new saucepan, OR, there goes my weekly Saturday jobs earnings. All the other girls thought it was hilarious. Relief that it was not them I am sure. A few curt words about not leaving cooking food unattended and that school insurance would pay for the saucepan alleviated my fear, but how do you explain not having the planned meal when you get home? I was saved that trauma by there being some spare potatoes to cook.

Sewing classes were much less dramatic to the point of being boring. I had excitedly agreed to make Mummy a skirt out of a piece of quite dreary greenish material she bought for me. Well, I could already sew and having to wait for the tutor to check every pattern layout and then inspect every seam sewn before allowing the garment to continue was enough to send me to sleep. When am I going to finish this, I thought to myself and totally lost interest. Dear Mummy never did get a completed skirt to wear! Patience was not my best virtue and has been one of the many life lessons to overcome. Many's the time when I would pray to God about something and "ask him in faith" but secretly wanting the answer "yesterday" please.

I could have learned patience and perseverance with the dreary greenish skirt material couldn't I? That is what brings about our goals, achievements and successes in life. The more we see lessons in the "dreary" times the greater person we become.

Chapter 8

Two Dogs, Two Budgerigars' and a Parrot

Childhood life was intermixed with joy through pets and others animals. Animals can be very therapeutic as we know now, with all the amazing work that is done with dogs that work with vulnerable groups such as the blind and disabled.

As a growing girl I recall our pet budgerigar called Peter whom I adored and taught to say a few words. He was allowed out to fly around and would settle on us and peck at our clothing and of course he would sit on Daddy's bald head – he lost most of his hair whilst in the Navy. A very intelligent little bird, a mixture of blues and greys in his feathers, he always seemed to know when Sylvia was due home from school and would tweet away at the appropriate time. When I changed schools from Secondary School to College I was later home because of the bus and train journey. Mummy would say to him "she won't be home yet it is only four o'clock. Peter learned four o'clock and would often take to talking away and say "Pretty four o'clock, pretty four o'clock!" much to our amusement.

Sometimes we would invite one of the ladies from Church round for a visit or we would go to her house. To me she seemed very "old fashioned" with longish clothes and not so fashionable shoes on her feet. Her hair was neatly plaited and wound around her head – very Edwardian style. I think this was all associated with the "getting saved" at the time when women were also expected to have long hair. This certainly was very long.

She also had a pet budgerigar. I cannot remember whether it was blue or green coloured but it had quite a collection of things to recite. It's debut performance one day was when it recited the whole of the 23rd Psalm! She had spent hours and hours teaching him and he performed to willing audiences.

A good deal less saintly than a budgerigar was the parrot that lived at the pet shop where I used to catch the bus home after shopping for Mummy in Hayes. Whilst waiting for the bus, all of a sudden from the pet shop came the most foul language that stopped passing shoppers in their tracks and was not really for the ears of a "Born Again Christian!" – every other word began with an "F". Where did it learn that one asks? Apparently the owners could not keep it because all visitors were politely greeted with "F*** Off!" Needless to say the pet shop took the parrot in and kept it in the kitchen at the back of the shop in the hopes it would stay quiet and just maybe forget the words. No chance! No way could it be sold. I wonder what did happen to the not so well spoken parrot? Perhaps it ended up in the "bird spirit world" doing penance?

Chapter 9

Will I make my Dream Come True?

My dream of a Nursing Career looms closer but first Sylvia must pass a minimum of four "O" levels to be accepted for the Nursing Course. The chosen chosen subjects include Biology and Human Anatomy, Physiology and Hygiene Determined to do well, Sylvia works hard at her studies which is a pleasure to do as it is a major step towards fulfilling the dream of becoming a qualified nurse. The Old Tin Hut still plays a major role in life and as the teenage hormones kick in I seem to be getting less infections.

Every Saturday and in School Holidays are taken up with a part time job in Woolworths Store in the next town – Southall. Sylvia was designated to a less than inspiring counter for a young girl – paints and polishes. We sold various paints and varnishes, paint types, simple home DIY products and good old fashioned bottled ammonia.

I knuckled down to the job and enjoyed the change of routine mixing with other than church people. Dedication to duty led to a rise in pay from 12 shillings and 6 pence (old money) to 12 shillings and 9 pence! Wow! I felt positively wealthy.

Soon after I begin working in Woolworth Asians started moving into Southall and would come into the store – ladies dressed in beautiful bright coloured Saris, the men in more Western style dress. A young lad about my age 14 – 15 yrs old regularly came in and seemed to make a rush for our counter. It was not long before we all realised he had a crush on Sylvia which was not reciprocated. Much teasing went on and I would keep an eye out for his approaching and make an excuse to do something under the counter so as not to be seen. Imagine telling Mummy and Daddy that I had been asked out by an Indian Lad who was of a totally different religious sect and certainly not "saved!"

Eventually he realised he was getting nowhere and there was no need for frequent ducking under the counter,

There was however a fateful day at Woolworths – a bit like the day at college when I nearly set the cookery room on fire. It was my duty to keep under the counter clean and dust free plus restock from under the counter as items were sold. One Saturday as I grabbed a bottle of ammonia to add to the counter display - Oh Gosh!!! It slipped from my hand and fell to the floor breaking into many pieces. Ammonia started to spread all over the floor and the stench of ammonia quickly rose upwards almost choking me and wafted across the store. I wished the floor would open up and swallow me. Temporarily I was moved to another counter but soon returned to "run" the counter as counter supervisor during the school holidays because I understood the products well. Much care was taken handling bottles I can tell you! We also sold various sizes of paint brushes – Harris make, as I remember and of good quality.

Like any other store Woolworth had its share of shoplifting but our counter did not seem to attract thieves – more interesting items to steal or was there? Imagine my surprise, when one Saturday afternoon a lady was browsing the counter whilst she dextrously slipped 1/2" and 1" paintbrushes up the sleeves of her coat! Brownie points given for being alert – no accounting for taste in shoplifting eh?

The proud income generator I was now, meant that I could make my own clothes and become more self-sufficient in my wardrobe. It was the expected thing anyway – "now you were earning money you must buy all your own clothes" Mummy said. 12 shillings and sixpence had to buy clothes, pay for any other goodies, birthdays and Christmas, plus money in the collection at The Old Tin Hut. I did somehow manage to save a little in a Post Office Savings account and proudly bought my first Peacock Blue Winter Coat from a shop in Southall run by a Jewish Lady. It was not cheap by the prices then but she let me have it for £4.10.00 (four pounds ten shillings). Mummy was with me to oversee my choice of course.

Life seemed to be going quite smoothly although my inner self was not totally happy and very shy around people. A bit ironic when, at work, I was cheery and chatted with colleagues and customers, overcoming my initial nervousness. So shy was Sylvia, that when visiting my church friends in the late teens, for a social get together in the evening, I would not ask where the washroom was and keep my legs crossed till I got home. I only spoke when approached and never lead a conversation. You see, I was always considered very well behaved as a growing child because I fell firmly into the old saying "Children should be seen and not heard" category. It was better to stay silent in ones own inner world than speak, act, and get into trouble. Not just with parents, but I so wanted to stay on the road to Heaven and not be sent to Hell!

One Sunday evening at Church it was announced that there was a major convention at Penygroes in Wales and it would be good to represent the Hayes Apostolic Church. Mummy and Daddy decided that we would all go – the accommodation was obviously very affordable and "The Lord would Provide" we were taught. That sealed it. No excuses about not going! I must add here that over the years of my journey I have certainly always been provided for – even in challenging times. Back then though I felt that it was more about "duty" to the faith.

So off we go to have some fun Praising God in Penygroes. The weather was kind to us for which I was very grateful, as I was to be baptised. This involved being immersed in a cold tank of water dressed in a long dark green gown – this ceremony meant that Sylvia would be fully confirmed as having committed to God as a "A Born again Christian" and then receive the gift of the Holy Spirit having symbolised ones commitment to the faith. Yes, I did find myself able to speak "Spirit" language as do many – not just Pentecostals. There was a good deal of singing including hymns and resounding Halleluiahs along with the Pentecostal Welsh Choir renderings. Then it was back home to readjust to daily life and questioning at college on where you had been for the week. I would hesitantly try to explain in embarrassed tones – I hated being so out of place with my peers.

Time is rapidly passing and studies to lead me to my Nursing Career are in full swing. Our lead Tutor was a "Miss" who had been a nurse and was very strict in her ways. She would bang on the desks to keep you awake and gave us a hard time with learning Human Biology and Hygiene.

Will I make my Dream Come True?

Questions would fly across the room accompanied with a look that filled you with raw fear if you could not answer her immediately.

"Oh Dear! She is going to ask me!" Fearfully, this thought runs through my mind. Sure it was - so I froze as she stared at me and shouted "Miss Bryden, What's up with you? Is your brain made of cauliflower?" The class giggled, I wanted to cry and someone else thankfully raised their hand and answered the question.

In hindsight I think I was being prepared for what was to come in my Nurse's Training. Another day we were being taught more about the human body and as I was concentrating to take it all in, my expression must have been of a sad, morose individual because once again I was picked on. *"Miss Bryden if you look like that when you are on the wards the patients will all drop dead!!!"* That was really inspiring for me - or not??!!! The irony of that particular statement she made is that when I **did** go into Nurse Training I was always the most popular one on the wards because I was happy and smiling.

The Pre-nursing course was co-educational, including both sexes. Here was a lad in our class who seemed very naive about many things especially girls monthly cycles. That was until we did the full anatomy of both sexes! There was one girl in the class who had very traumatic menstruation manifestation with acute nausea and even vomiting. One particular day she was overcome with this and was to be seen draped over a wash basin in the classroom trying desperately not to "throw up". Our good classmate, Mr Naivity asked what was wrong, trying to show some concern. "It's my monthly" was the response from over the sink. "Oh! I understand!" Mr Naivity immediately empathetically droned "I get that too!" The girls went into hysterical laughter which Mr Naivity could not understand. It even seemed to perk up the nauseous figure draped over the basin!

In spite of the disapproving comments made in class I succeeded in passing the required "O" Levels and going on to start my Nursing Career.

One of the statutory subjects was English Literature and Shakespeare was always included in the exam. Macbeth was the play we had to know in depth. Soon there was to be another challenge facing Sylvia, who spent nearly all of her leisure time at that place affectionately – or not – known as "The old Tin Hut".

Tutor announces that to help us with our revision for English Literature, a trip had been organised to see a performance of the play at London's famous Old Vic Theatre where many famous stars are proud to act out their desire to have a part in a Shakespeare play. Sylvia feels elated at the prospect of going to London *and* the famous Theatre. Soon the elation is followed by the pain of fear in her gut – we have to get permission to go just like the pictures all those years ago. "At least I can say it will help with my GCE exam" the thought quickly rises up! Sylvia waited till the very last moment before deadline, for booking before a request is put in to go. The elephant sized tummy butterflies are rearing up with a dry mouth for fear of being told "No you cannot!" It took great persuasion but a positive response eventually given. Quite a breakthrough in facing fear and being persistent so as to achieve my goal here! Hereby hangs the tale of yet another experience.....

The day dawned and all was set for us to take the trip to the Old Vic. Sylvia travelled with classmates and felt elated at actually doing something away from the rigid "Old Tin Hut" routine. The play was riveting to watch and helped make sense of the plot in readiness for the exams. Then it was that the evening took a different turn. The journey home resulted in arrival at Northolt Station with a bus ride to the end of our street to get home. Mummy and Daddy had an expected time of arrival as 11pm, latest. As we came out of the station there was an extremely thick fog and difficulty to see across the road. My friends were picked up by car and Sylvia was left stranded to get the bus. No offer of a lift was forthcoming. The car disappeared into the fog and hope for the last bus arose within. Standing at the bus stop was a gentleman also waiting for the bus. Eventually it seemed that there was to be no bus turn up! "it looks like they have cut out the last bus" said the gentleman "Where do you live?" "Off Yeading Lane" I nervously replied. "I'm going that way and will see you home safely" he responded with a kind voice. We set off and he led me through the dense fog to the end of our street. He was indeed an angel and just chatted and had a fatherly attitude about him. When I eventually arrived home The greeting was far from pleasant "Where do you think you have been?" Mummy roared I explained what had happened as best I could – "You walked home with a strange man! You could have been attacked or raped!" she cried. Daddy then stepped in "Calm down Elsie! She is at least home safely and no harm has come to her!" Gradually they both calmed down and seemed relieved that I had arrived safely back. Of course, in all the turmoil, I wasn't asked how the play went; just sent to bed, so that I would be up in time for college the next day. These days we would have our mobile phone with us and make contact. Modern technology sure has it's blessings!

Exam time came and all subjects were successfully passed in spite of the regular instructions to complete homework in time for the prayer meeting! Perhaps God and the Angels helped as I was faithful in my attendance? Or was it my determination to get into nurse training?

I was accepted to do a joint nurse training commencing with Orthopaedic Nursing which would be followed by General Nursing. A long way from the four year old who was not expected to make anything of herself!

Determination to succeed will always overcome fear and adversity, however long and winding the road may be, to achieving steps to our final goal.

My time at College and part time work had helped me begin to integrate in the world at large, but little did I know what was ahead of me as I prepared to leave here and step into the big wide world of medicine. A truly daunting prospect along with the excitement of being closer to fulfilling the dream of a child!

Later on in life Sylvia was to realise the value of a good coach/mentor to help with the journey of change and to be prepared to "BE YOURSELF" and "LIVE OUT WHO YOU TRULY ARE".

PART 2

A Dream Comes True – Tales From the Nursing Years

Chapter 1

Was I prepared for the shock?

October 1960 - Sylvia had reached the age of 17 years and 3 months of age precisely.

After the overwhelming joy at being accepted for a joint Nurse Training programme, the reality of it had now arrived. Up until now life had revolved very much around study and the Old Tin Hut interspaced with regular "Convention Weekends". To say it was a sheltered life would be putting it mildly! The only real interaction with "worldly people" was my part time job in Woolworths plus College days.

The day dawns for me to pack my bags and move into the nursing home at the Royal National Orthopaedic Hospital in Stanmore. I was both excited and nervous about launching forth into the unknown. Mummy was pleased for me, Daddy proud that his favourite little girl was embarking on her career at last. I would of course return home on my "days off" for which I would give the calculated amount of money to Mummy as my "home board". This was because we were refunded money in our salary for the days we were not boarding at the hospital. Being unaware at that time of the financial restraints at home I resented this, as all my colleagues in my "training set" got to keep theirs. Later reflection made me realise that it was a good lesson in budgeting and paying your way in the big wide world.

On arrival at R N O H Stanmore I joined my colleagues in the old House next to the entrance gate which were the living quarters along with with the preliminary training facilities. Back then there were strict rules regarding our living quarters with only two passes per week for staying out late.

The initiation into our training included this information and we were to share rooms whilst living in this house. The Tutor and "Home Sister" as they were known paired us up with a roommate and showed us to our rooms. Still very shy, the thought of sharing a room filled me with fear and trepidation. No turning back now Sylvia! Sink or Swim time! Uniforms were handed out – we had filled in forms with height, weight and dress size weeks before. Regulation shoes were insisted upon. Practical, hardwearing and supportive black lace up style had to be purchased. It was good old "Clarks" as I recall. Uniform was a pale blue dress with a separate stiff collar to attach plus elasticated waist belt. Having sent in measurements meant that we all had a dress that was 12 inches (30 cms) from the floor. The collars were not pleasant to wear and often rubbed against the skin causing red areas to appear from friction, but we just had to grin and bear it. Caps were worn with pride – different styles for students and trained staff.

Initial training begins the very next morning with uniform inspection and of course our hair. The ruling was short hair, no makeup or earrings and anyone whose hair had grown to almost on the collar would be strictly ordered "up or off Nurse!" Shoes had to be clean at all times and around the grounds we were allowed to wear a navy blue cardigan and navy blue cape with red lining. This was worn on cold days, especially as there was a long walk from the nursing home to ward blocks. Strictly no cardigans to be worn on the wards – even in wintertime. Training was very practical and we learned basic procedures like bed making to begin with – this was very "military" as duvets had not been invented. Special "hospital" corners with starched bed sheets initially was the routine and the top sheet had to be turned down 18" (37.5 cms). Pillows were shaken and set with the open end facing away from the door and finally a blue counterpane – heavy duty cotton cover was applied with great precision so that the mitred corners neatly hung down at each side. We girls mostly wore stockings with suspender belts (tights were yet to fully hit the market). Metal suspenders were a definite danger to bed making. Many a time I would get an electric shock as suspenders "pinged" against the side of the bed and static electricity bounced from the bed to suspender. Sometimes it was quite painful and left a mark! A quiet "Ouch!" was uttered frequently.

Was I prepared for the shock?

We learned how to do basic observations with a good old mercury filled thermometer reading in Fahrenheit temperature and pulse check was by hand. To a novice, finding a pulse spot in the wrist was not easy – how on earth do Chinese herbalists find six pulses around the wrist I often wondered to myself as I was struggling to find one! No digital machines or disposable thermometers then! Blood Pressure readings were again carried out with a mercury filled apparatus attached to a wrap round cotton arm cuff plus stethoscope which was carefully placed over the mainlood vessel in the anterior region of the elbow joint. Now one had to carefully keep this in place with one hand while the other dextrously pumped up the cuff and slowly release air within the cuff and read the mercury gradients on the apparatus. Good hearing was also required to hear when pressure sounds began and ended. This indicated the reading which was the carefully charted on the patients observation chart.

After six weeks of practicing on dummies of bathing, bedpan techniques and setting up a trolley for sterile procedures, we were let loose on the wards to work on real patients. Again this is a "sink or swim" time for Sylvia especially as she is designated to an adult male ward.

The wards were "Nissan" huts used during World War II pristinely converted for patient care with beds in rows on either side. In winter they could be a little chilly and draughty – "I wish I was allowed to wear my cardigan!" but rules were to be strictly adhered to or the wrath of Matron would be upon you!

I was rostered for the late shift on my first day and walked the long corridor – open to all elements in between the wards with only a roof to hold back some of the rain or snow. Proudly I walked on to the ward in my uniform, complete with brand new fob watch and name tag adorning my dress. I hung my cape up and gingerly knocked on the office door "Come in" the Ward Sisters voice responded – "Welcome! It's Nurse Bryden isn't it? "That's right" I replied hiding my nerves fluttering in my abdomen – fear and excitement combined. A full report was given by the nurse in charge of the morning shift and then duties were delegated to those of us on until 10.00 p.m. I was designated a nurse to shadow me but was to be thrown in at the deep end too.

"Nurse Bryden, will you take a bedpan to Mr Jones at the end on the right?" Something within me froze with embarrassment – only in biology lessons had I seen pictures of the male anatomy. I was about to see my first fully naked male body in a spinal plaster bed for those who have spinal surgery as they do not wear pyjamas – just covered with a sheet for warmth and decency. Bravely I marched down the ward with a pristine clean stainless steel bedpan you could see your face in, covered with a bedpan cover cloth.

"Hello I'm Nurse Bryden" I state, pulling the curtains around the bed. "Whey Hey!" a male voice cries "You're lucky having a good looking young nurse behind the curtains with you" I clung to the bedpan trying not to show my embarrassment and gingerly pulled back the bedclothes to place the bedpan strategically in the correct position. Trying not to be seen to be staring. "Ring the bell when you are ready" I stated and removed myself from behind the curtains. "Nurse I need a bedpan too" echoed around the ward from the other patients with big grins on their faces. I was already learning that patients easily recognise "new recruits" and love to tease and make fun of them. I realised that I had to very quickly learn how to deal with this and fortunately more senior students always backed me up. Ward experience having began, we took the preliminary exam after the first six weeks classroom training. Thankfully we all passed this with flying colours!

Training continued with combined theory in the classroom and practical experience on the wards. As time passed I became more able to deal with challenging patients and retort back in fun and my confidence began to grow. The uniform helped too. It was like putting on a protective shield and confidence dress. A useful tip for all areas of life – dress in clothes that make you look good. Wear bright positive colours and you will begin to feel happier and confident. To attract success - dress for success even around the home.

Chapter 2

No Excuses!

The next challenge I vividly recall is my very first experience of working on Night Duty Shifts. Here is a seventeen and a half year old having stepped from the cocoon of a restricted life being thrown into responsibility for other lives. Somehow I was doing well and my faith in the Master Jesus seemed to be carrying me through. I did pray every night and morning and gained strength and comfort from this. My nominated ward for Night Duty Shift was a children's ward with patients from a few months old to around 10 years of age. Being an Orthopaedic Hospital babies and young children would be admitted for surgery and medical treatment for birth defects such as dislocated hips which needed splinting in plaster for a number of months, to others going through a series of operations to allow various deformities to be rectified as best as possible. If the children were not totally bedridden they spent most of the day in a wheelchair or "rushing around" on crutches - the speed they could get up on a pair of wooden crutches was amazing to watch. Wheelchair speed races were also popular if they could get away with it.

A very prompt 10.00 p.m. Night Shift awaits me – or should I say 09.45 p.m. arrival for a detailed report for 28 patients to care for by myself with an auxiliary nurse/carer helping myself and another ward. That would be unheard of in this century but we just had to get on with it with grit and determination – I look at my list of things to be done overnight and begin after a quick presentation. In a one bedded cubicle next to the office is a child who has had hip surgery and required, as I had been told at report, "quarter hourly observations" which meant that every 15 minutes during the night in amongst every other task required to be carried out, I would check the pulse, respirations, blood pressure plus observe the dressing over the operation site for signs of bleeding and make sure the catheter tube from the bladder was draining urine into the bottle beside the bed. Oh yes, a sterile bottle indeed! Disposable drainage bag systems had not yet come our way – even blood transfusions were still administered through tubing that required "milking" occasionally to keep the blood dripping though. Yet another bottle had to be checked which was draining excess fluid from the operation site. It was quite daunting to a not quite 18 year old young woman thrust into the career she had dreamed of all those years ago. Luckily all the children were sleeping and breathing normally. My next task was to write up a full report to be taken to the Night Superintendent by midnight. This consisted of a hand written statement regarding all 28 patients in an A4 ruled book, continuing on from the day nurses reports. When I say a "Statement" I mean, each patient had to have written down their full name, age, the diagnosis of the condition that they had been admitted with, the surgeon whom they were registered with PLUS ALL previous operations including the date on which they had occurred. THEN we could write a short statement about their general condition on that day! "Well" I thought to myself "this is interesting! All I know of them is that they are lying asleep in their bed and seem to be OK, no pain, and breathing!" Anything more than that was almost guess work!

Meticulously every 15 minutes I do the "observations" of the post-operative child and am aware that time is ticking away for the Midnight Report to be delivered to Night Sister's Office. At 3 minutes to midnight the phone rings – "Nurse Bryden where is your report?" the voice angrily shouts in my ear "It is my first night Sister, and I have a post-operative child on quarterly observations" I nervously respond". That's no excuse" she retorts "I want your report on my desk by midnight" – Thankfully I call the ward next door and request the auxiliary nurse to come and collect it for me, struggling to complete it within two minutes ensuring neatly underlined and key information about each patient – "Don't worry Nurse Bryden" the auxiliary nurse says reassuringly "She's a bit of an old cow – we all know what she can be like. Just make sure that by 2.00 a.m. when she does her full round on the ward that you know <u>ALL</u> the information about any patient as she will expect you to know it by then!"

When she left I made myself a drink and began learning everything about the children in my charge. The "runner" nurse as we called them because they would "run" between two wards helping with turning patients and the early morning routine – returned and I was allowed an hour supper break in the night canteen that served cooked meals for us. I was glad of some "breathing space" but inside petrified about the dreaded "2.00 a.m. Round" with Night Sister.

All was well on my return and I continued my duty to my many tasks. Just before 2.00 a.m. the phone rings – it is the ward next door "She's on her way" a voice whispers down the phone. Nervously I have a last memory recall and wait for Night Sisters appearance. The ward door opens and in walks a tall female figure in Navy Blue Uniform, cape adoring her and crisply starched white cap on her head. I stood up and greeted her "Good Morning Sister" "Good Morning Nurse Bryden – shall we go round the ward now?" "Certainly Sister" My mouth is parched with fear of not remembering all that I should but somehow I managed to get everything correct and even got a "Well Done Nurse Bryden" from "The Old Cow". As soon as she left my ward I hurried to the phone and dialled the number of the next ward "She's on the way" I whispered down the phone and replaced the receiver quietly.

The report book had been returned by Night Sister and at around 5.00 a.m. it was time to write the report for the day staff which would indicate how well each child had slept. A small gap was left to fill in with any specific changes noted during the morning routine after waking the children.

Before I knew it, 6 a.m. dawns and then it is a mad rush to complete the required tasks by 07.30 a.m. when the day duty staff would arrive. Babies to be fed and nappies changed – all children washed and dressed and in their wheelchairs. Medication to be administered plus breakfast served. All this for 28 children to be completed in one and a half hours, as well as the special observations every 15 minutes. The "runner" auxiliary would help as well thankfully. I hand over keys and give a report to the day staff at 7.30 a.m. leaving the ward exhausted to go for a snack in the canteen then it is back to my room for a relaxing bath and into bed for some sleep before repeating the routing again. My belly clock did not like night shifts and I was challenged with sleeping during the day. With such a lot to do during the night tiredness went unnoticed and a good adrenaline seemed to kick in thankfully.

As the night shifts continue I am able to deal with the laborious tasks assigned each night and get myself really organised and even manage to finish the "hour and a half" routine before 07.30 am!

CHAPTER 3

The Grey Lady, A Cow and Sticky Floors

OH DEAR! I am in my second year of training, I am rostered for night duty again and this time it is on the incubation ward where each patient has their own room because they have conditions that require treating infections. It was crucial in orthopaedics that any sign of infection was treated as a Major incident for the patient and they were immediately put in isolation until it healed. This time I had a colleague working with me which made the night routine a lot easier. With young men as patients one had to be on your guard if they took a fancy to you which did happen of course! One can be vulnerable shut in a small room with a male patient! Because the night routine was less hectic on this ward we had "extra" duties to carry out. Unlike today where sterile packs of dressings came pre-done and ready to use they were put together in a Central Sterilisation Unit and packed in stainless steel drums which were then loaded into large sterilising chambers and sterilised by heat. Each day a dressing drum was delivered to each ward for daily dressing procedures. Our task at night was to carefully create gauze squares and cotton wool balls and pack them into empty sterilising drums ready for collection next morning. The report book came in very useful here. It was the perfect dimension for wrapping round the gauze from a large roll. The gauze would then be cut through at each side of the book and produce a pile of perfect sized gauzes which we then meticulously folded into small squares and packed neatly into the stainless steel drum. A bit like medical origami! Cotton wool balls had to be a certain size and production was speedy as all drums delivered had to be ready by morning. There was one more night duty experience during Sylvia's Orthopaedic Nurse Training which was way down the back of the grounds. It was always said to be "out in the sticks" and was a cold walk during winter. Even the long heavy cape did not keep out the cold. This ward was a convalescent unit with all ages being placed here – mainly children and babies in for recuperation after major surgery on the wards. Being rostered here caused much gossip as there were vivid tales of "The Grey Lady" who walked around and then stood looking into one of the cots as if there was a baby in there she knew. It happened mostly in the month of October and I can only deduce now that the baby must have passed over in this month. Guess what month Sylvia was to work there? Yes! October! My Pentecostal upbringing was very clear on not acknowledging "ghosts" or communicating with "the dead". After all the tales of the Grey Lady I had butterflies as big as elephants when arriving for duty. Being a large unit and way out in the wilds there were two nurses rostered to cover this unit – thank goodness! Fortunately I never actually saw the Grey Lady, but walking round during the night to check patients with just a torch to light the way was a bit scary I can tell you! Any noise and the hairs on the back of the neck stood up and goose bumps appeared on your arms. Because of the location of the ward we were advised to call the back gate porter if at all concerned, and one night we had to do just that. It was around 3.00 a.m. and pitch black darkness outside. My colleague and I were sitting in the office having a cup of tea when we heard a noise outside the window as if someone was knocking on the window. We both froze in our seats, mouths dry with fear and neither of us wanted to go out and investigate – might be a druggy wanting to get in or a burglar. After a couple of minutes we decided it was a good idea to call the night porter. He contacted security and told us to stay exactly where we were and try to keep calm. Security arrived and came into the office with big grins from ear to ear as we sat terrified in our chairs. "You know there is a farm next door to this end of the hospital?" One of them said. "Yes" we answered nervously. "Well" replied his colleague "One of the cows escaped and was standing outside the office window- what you were hearing was its tail banging on the window!" they were now laughing their heads off and we felt SO stupid. "I'll put the kettle on" I said and we all indulged in tea and biscuits and laughed together. I bet they had a good laugh with their mates back at security base. What with the "Grey Lady" and the "escaped cow" incident I was relieved to go back on day duty again. Generally day duty was fairly uneventful and I was growing in confidence daily and doing well in tests until..........

I am this time, rostered for the teenagers ward managed by a very efficient Senior Male Charge Nurse with a good sense of humour and discipline – with teenagers this was essential. Stuck in hospital for up to 3 months away from home brought out some interesting behaviour from them – the boys especially. The boys somehow took a shine to Sylvia and we would have a good banter and my sense of humour and "wind up" character emerged here. Many of them were in wheelchairs during the day and would have races up and down the ward (when charge nurse was not around) – we nurses joined in and I was quite adept at wielding a wheelchair after a little practice! There was a lovely Downs Syndrome lad on the ward and he was always asking Charge Nurse "Do you like Nurse Bryden?" "Are you going to marry her?" Charge Nurse would give same apt response and I would suitably blush and find something to do to recover my embarrassment. Looking back on this particular ward experience it really did make me take charge of myself and become assertive! No way could one for even a second allow the kids to get the better of you. There I was around 19 yrs of age, from a cocooned, restricted childhood thrust into a surrrogate Nurse/Mother of a load of vibrant teenagers who were bored with having to be in hospital. Somewhere deep within was all that I needed to deal with the challenges I was to face, yet then I was not fully aware of it.

Charge Nurse grilled all new students as soon as they arrived on the word "You HAVE to be tough and strong here and never ever let them get the better of you otherwise they will run rings around you. You must find a way of gaining their respect from the minute you stop onto the ward". Talk about a great lesson for "Face the Fear and Do It Anyway"! There was certainly little choice in this situation. Somehow I seemed to develop an insensitive skill of discipline and compromise with the boys especially. Although primarily day duty I did do some night shifts and I recall one in particular:-

Disposable plastic syringes had just been introduced into hospitals which was great BUT Oh boy! Not so on our ward! I walked onto the boys ward around 10 p.m. after taking report and to my horror there they all were – supposed to be asleep – playing syringe fights filled with liquid. Somehow they had removed the syringes from the rubbish bin. Not just water but orange drink!!! I got splattered and as I walked on the floor the sound of shoes catching on syrup like droplets was happening. To make things worse, the flooring was of polished wood that had been mopped and polished with a rotary electric polishing machine every day. Holy Moses!!! What would Charge Nurse say in the morning – What was I to tell him? "OK – Stop that right now!" I roared standing to my full height of 5ft 2 ¾ inches "You do realise that I will have to tell the Charge Nurse in the morning. The flooring is ruined and has to be cleaned and polished!" Silence for a few seconds. "Right! Here's the deal – give me all your syringes NOW! I will clean the floor and polish it and will say nothing to Charge Nurse but you MUST NEVER do this again – do you hear?" Genuinely subdued, some of them in angst giggles, apologised. I had also to consider we had a report to write by 12.00 midnight PLUS Night Sister would be round at maximum 2 a.m. for her round. We did not dare turn the full lights on as they would be seen from the outside. So with baited breath I proceeded to clean and polish the floor and Centre Aisle polished wood storage unit in almost darkness, making sure that not a trace of orange drink was anywhere. In spite of the "extra work" everything went smoothly and neither Night Sister nor Charge Nurse found out – if they suspected anything, nothing was ever said.

Working with polio victims and children with other congenital deformities made one very grateful for everything you were able to do with your life and times. On the girls ward was a young girl of around 11 years of age who could write, draw and knit with her toes! She was always cheerful and never complained. How many times do we take things for granted in life, really appreciate even the basic things in life? Here I was, still at a young age learning major life lessons that still touch my heart as I write.

Being a teenage ward there was of course music played all day long unless any of them were away at teaching classes. Songs of Adam Faith, Elvis Presley and other chart hits of the early1960's resounded around the ward daily. Being a famous hospital sometimes a famous singer visited one of their dedicated fans and we did have a visit from one of them. Adam Faith it was, if memory serves me correctly. The favourite most days was "What do you want?" - Much as I loved Adam Faith's songs and still do now, I have to say, hearing the same song blaring out every day did get a bit much sometimes. It was a relief to hear a bit of Elvis Presley or Cliff Richard for a change. They were top of my list as pop stars. I even got to see Cliff at Wembley during his more mature years and his energy and great performance was still present. I also lived in Cliff's home town for a few years and recall singing carols with him and others around the Christmas Tree on the evening of switching on the Christmas lights. Overall, I enjoyed my time on the teenagers ward and it's challenges.

Chapter 4

Off with his leg! – GO!

From the teenage turmoil, Sylvia was now to have yet another challenge being sent to work in the operating theatre and would now experience bodies being cut open with the intent of repairing damaged joints and spines.

I arrived for my first shift and was given rigorous training on how to dress for being in the sterile operating room environment. Suitably dressed and wearing white clogs, I am taken into the operating theatre to observe the morning operations. It was like walking into a sterile carpentry workshop! There were two stainless steel trolleys draped in dark green sterile cloth adorned with saws, hammers, chisels, drill and drill bits and a collection of various screws and screwdrivers. Of course Orthopaedic Surgery is a bit like carpentry but inside the body is isn't it? Replacing hip joints, fixing damaged spines and other joints will involve sawing off bits of bone and replacing with metal substitutes and replacement joint bones that need screwing in place. My job was to pick up the gauze squares that were used by the surgeons and hang them on a dedicated rack for counting at the end of the operation before the final sutures were put into ensure that we had the same number we started with. Sometimes the surgeon would drop a blood stained swab and it would "disappear" only to be retrieved with great dexterity on my part from his wellington boot! Orthopaedic Surgeons vary in character and one was renowned for his shouting orders in a military like fashion to the Nurses accompanying him. I would cringe in my clogs for fear of being on the receiving end of his tongue also. Thankfully it never happened.

There was a Theatre Porter who kept spirits up with his sense of humour which was sometimes a little bit over the top. I recall one day we had a patient on the operating list for a below knee leg amputation. I did not relish having to witness this, but of course had to grit my teeth and overcome any apprehension, and get on with my tasks. After the leg had been successfully amputated it was passed to the Theatre Porter to dispose of in a special bin. As he tossed the limb into the bin he shouted "Anyone want roast leg for Sunday Lunch?" I felt sick as laughter rang out from the other staff but maybe that was how he coped with such drastic surgical procedures. I adjusted to the typical "Theatre" atmosphere – even the language that sometimes spewed out of the mouths of the consultants as they cleaned certain instruments for the next part of the operation procedure. Unheard of at "The Old Tin Hut" in Hayes and of course a sin to utter even any minor profanities. Eeh! Was I certainly having a major life awakening on my nursing career path! Looking back though, all these experiences were preparation for my ensuing life purpose to truly be able to help others Knowledge PLUS experiences is the best university to graduate from. Many of the world's top speakers and motivators backgrounds are "life experience!"

Time passes with more practical learning along with lots of hard work committing to memory all the bones and muscles in the body, so that we know them in our heads and can apply to our nursing. Somewhere in the dark depths of my brain is the knowledge, but ask me to recite any little bone in the wrist and ankles, all the muscles everywhere in the body from face to foot – I might be a little bit challenged! However, when knowledge is needed sometimes to help somebody the "computer programme" comes up trumps for me.

I stayed in the Nurses Quarters for this training apart from my days off when I went home and joined the Church Circle temporarily. There was a great camaraderie between myself and the nurses who started with me and we would meet up during off duty times in someone's room for merriment and Cider. Now Sylvia was being introduced to another "sin" and fully "let loose" duly indulged till my head and stomach reminded me I was not used to this the next morning but that made no difference! We had to make sure "Home Sister" who was like a strict mother to us did not get wind of what we were up to and always had someone keeping an eye out in case she suddenly appeared.

One particular day we were enjoying ourselves in someone's room and one of the girls was using her bed as a trampoline. Suddenly there was a loud crack, the bed base snapped and she was thrown into the air. Everyone was laughing hysterically and then we realised we had to do something about it. We did not dare tell Home Sister as it would result in a severe disciplinary and being sent to Matron. That was a <u>major</u> in my training days – like the military. One of the girls instantly had an inspiration – "there's a spared bed base in the store cupboard down the corridor" she related with excitement. "What we do is this – one keep guard and divert Home Sister's attention while the rest of us swop over the beds. She'll never know!" "Brilliant" we all cried out. The plan went smoothly despite nervous fear of seeing Home Sister.

It was fun in spite of the discipline and being at ground floor level in the Nurses Quarter facilitated a rota system for those who were out in the evening and wanted to sneak in late past the Night Porter. Whoever was on the Late Night shift had to leave their bedroom window open so that whoever was out late could climb in. One of the girls was a keen "indoor gardener" with her windowsill filled with a variety of potted plants. Many a night I would be woken at 2.00 a.m. in the morning with a loud bang as plant pots fell to the floor whilst a colleague sneaked in once more.

Well, soon I would be moving to the next phase of my Nurses Training and it was time to have to pick one of the London Hospitals where I would complete my General Nursing. It was a choice of The Middlesex Hospital or Hammersmith Hospital for me and I was accepted to go to Hammersmith. I was delighted as I would experience greatly from mixed hospital procedures up to the latest research treatment and witness pioneering surgery etc.

The Royal National Orthopaedic Hospital established many Orthopaedic Nursing Hospital Trends and time has passed enjoying the training in a world renowned environment. Suddenly it seemed the Orthopaedic Nursing Certificate Exams loomed before me. All free time was spent revising to ensure we all knew all had absorbed all we possibly could absorb to get through the exams. Many hours were spent with Sylvia helping a colleague remember the small bones of the wrist and ankle with rhymes and we were proud of our memories. The Hospital Finals Exam day arrived and with a stomach full of butterflies as big as elephants I did my best and felt had done well. "If only I can come top in the exam" I thought "My dream of 4 years of age is now becoming a reality" I was excited at the thought of proudly receiving my award for this.

Time passed and both exams were completed. Hospital Final Results were given first and my dear friend who I had been helping with revision came in first, beating me by two marks. I was initially gutted but then knew that I had done my very best and was 2nd place and only 3 marks off first place. I had at least aimed for top marks and worked hard. I went home elated at my achievement against all childhood challenges and proudly told Mummy and Daddy my results only to be told "Well, it's a shame you didn't come first!" – like a knife that was plunged into my heart and the words went deep. Sensitive Sylvia went on another major guilt trip that impacted greatly on many years of my life. Those few words went straight to the subconscious programming of the brain and from that day on I always had to "do better" no matter how well I was doing.

It was many years later that I realised that it was great to always strive to do better but not from a phasing guilt trip, but a desire to win. There is a great difference between being inspired to better our ability to achieve success and acting from guilt and fear. To be inspired by inner belief in our dreams and ability to succeed, serves us well in life and brings inner joy and peace. It is a habit worth pursuing.

Well, Sylvia did pick herself up and there was much rejoicing when she was formally accepted into Hammersmith Hospital fully, successfully passing exams that gave her the Orthopaedic Nursing Certificate Qualification.

Although the official qualification certificate would not be valid until Sylvia completed her General Nurse Training, there was a celebration and award ceremony held at the hospital to which family members were invited. A celebrity was always invited to present the certificates and awards. Our chosen celebrity was to be the famous Michael Flanders of the duo performers Flanders and Swan. Wheelchair bound, he had spent a great deal of time at the RNOH as a patient in his earlier years. The day dawned for the ceremony as Sylvia was coming to the end of a Night Duty shift on a very warm summer's day. It would be important to get some sleep beforehand and as the weather was really warm with blue skies, I decided to rest outside the nurse's home on the grass. When I awoke from a deep sleep with the sun pouring down my face felt really warm. On looking in the mirror on my return to my room I viewed a bright red face. "Oh My Goodness!" I thought "What can I do? I have to go up on the stage and meet Michael Flanders this afternoon!" Applications of cold flannels didn't seem to help the red face either. Oh well, nothing to do except get on with getting a pristine uniform prepared and polish the shoes to a deep shine and get ready.

As I had come second in the hospital finals I was to receive a prize which I eagerly awaited. The venue was a large hall complete with a stage in the original old house where the annual Christmas concert would take place. When my name was called, I proudly walked up to the stage of the large hall to meet Michael Flanders. He of course noticed my red face which was even redder with embarrassment and commented with a smile "I see we have been enjoying the sun today" as he shook hands and presented my prize – "Congratulations on doing so well!" I was filled with emotion and joy at having achieved part of my dream and went to sit down with my colleagues. The award didn't overly excite me – a copy of a book called "Shakespeare and Medicine" which discussed his many plays and sonnets and their mentions of medical matters. I have kept the book as a memory but have never read it from cover to cover. Probably because I am not a dedicated fan of Shakespeare!

My thoughts turn now to the Annual Christmas concerts and one of them stands out as really hilarious. The consultants and postgraduate student doctors always took part throwing themselves into the spirit of things with great gusto! How they found time to practice I'll never know, but the performance was always perfect for amateurs! It was their turn to come on stage and everyone was waiting to see what they had conjured up. The curtains opened and on stage paraded very butch doctors clad in bright yellow bikinis with black spots on! They then proceeded to cavort about the stage in a pathetic attempt to look like sexy "drag artists" whilst miming to the then popular song, Yellow Polka Dot Bikini! Well, suffice it to say they brought the house down!! Very difficult to follow that act!!

CHAPTER 5

THE NEXT STEP
"Inmates" Over the Wall!

THE RNOH, ALTHOUGH spread far and wide was not a "big" hospital in terms of patient numbers that were catered for. I recall the interview at Hammersmith hospital, before being accepted and Matron warning me that it was a much larger Hospital than the Orthopaedic at Stanmore and would take some adjusting to. I assured her that I would cope and wanted to be a part of the training scheme – courage springing up again to face another new challenge. However, to progress in life we must face challenges head on. The road to success is paved with many challenges from which we learn to grow. In a few days a letter arrived at home and I nervously open it as Mummy reminds me that if it is God's will, I will be accepted. Joy oh Joy! I am accepted and Mummy excitedly measures me and we complete the Uniform form along with my signature signing my acceptance. I am to commence training the first week of March 1963 which will last 2 ½ years.

Hammersmith Hospital is another world renowned institute where research into revolutionary clinical techniques are constantly being explored. I felt privileged to be part of such a place. In fact during the time of Sylvia's training, to say that you had qualified as a Nurse at one of the six London Hospitals was a great accolade and credibility for any job application.

There was little time for "adjustment" on arrival and it was very much "in the deep end" as a second year student. The Nursing Home was typical of it's time – long corridors of rooms and bathrooms and a small kitchen for making drinks on each floor. Strict rules applied – no men of any description were allowed in your own room even your father. Home Sister who oversaw things was a strict "dedicated discipline" and combined her role as Nurse Tutor. Once again there were very strict "late night" rules and only two late passes (after 10.00 p.m.) per week were allowed. Of course many nurses got away with it and like the RNOH the Night Porter would chuckle and ask for more creative names than "Smith" or "Jones" from those who tried it on regularly. Sylvia was still a bit of a "goody two shoes" and any evenings out were usually church related and never went over the time limit. With strict discipline revolving around visitors to the nursing home we would spend time entertaining ourselves in each other's bedrooms. As the evening progressed Nursing Home Sister/Tutor would do a round to check we were all in our room and not getting up to mischief. Sometimes opening the door to peak in. If a number of us were all gathered in one room and Sister was on the prowl, as we heard her coming, a moments panic set in, plus giggles and one of us would hide under the bed and two others cram themselves in the wardrobe trying not to laugh. The door knocks and Sister peers in – "All OK Nurse? Time for lights out now!" "Yes Sister" was the response trying not to laugh. Bodies appear from under the bed and in the wardrobe. Listening carefully and giving Home Sister time to disappear, everyone returns to their own room to bed down for the night.

Sometimes, nurses in my "set" and others would pass the evening away by making a sort of "weegie" board with alphabet letters on paper placed in a circle on a table and an upturned glass, Sylvia disapproved of this due to her upbringing and only once sat in and watched out of curiosity. There was to be a test the next day and one of them requested that they call a spirit and ask what the test was to be about. All agreed and sure enough the glass did begin to go to letters at great speed and spell out the word "Blood". "Please be more specific" one of them annoyingly responded. With lightning speed the word "blood" was spelt out again and the glass rapidly moved to the edge of the table and nearly fell to the floor. A third attempt for more information only received the same response so the session was brought to a close. The next all went into the classroom for the

THE NEXT STEP: "Inmates" Over The Wall!

test and there were gasps and holding of breath as the tutor wrote on the blackboard – **Please write down all you know about blood.**

Sessions continued and I did not sit and watch any more but received "reports" of what happened. This practice came to an abrupt end after a spirit predicted a nurses pending ill heath which actually happened and sadly she died before completing her training!! Who the spirit was, I never found out, but knew it would not be a very enlightened one as they are usually sensitive to how they bring messages through – Sylvia was to learn this later in life as her spiritual calling unfolded.

The Nurses Home was positioned so that you were on the second or third floor and one had a good view of Wormwood Scrubs Prison which is right next door to the Hospital. Warnings were given about undressing in front of the window with the curtains being drawn across so as not to "disturb" the inmates! I recall vividly being able to see one inmate quite clearly from my window who always seemed to have a pair of dark grey socks adorning the bars across his window. I often wondered what he was doing time for as "The Scrubs" as it is affectionately known was a very high security prison.

If an inmate needed hospitalisation we were the nominated hospital – not far to travel! We are given strict instructions when on the wards regarding the handling of these patients as often there were admitted due to swallowing cutlery items so that they could escape via the hospital. A security guard was with them at all times – well nearly all the time – "natural" breaks would be required from time to time of course! That was when an innocent very junior nurse was a sitting target for the prisoner. "Nurse can I use the phone please?" Not thinking, nurse would bring the phone trolley to the bedside and in seconds the call was made, the escape plan was ready to execute on next security guard's "Natural Break". Occasionally it worked and a red faced junior nurse would be suitably disciplined for being stupid enough to allow them to use the telephone! The hospital was also a great "route" to the outside world and working on Casualty on a night shift was occasionally "extra" interesting. Suddenly policeman and police dogs would appear as if from nowhere and we were warned that a dangerous prisoner had escaped. Interestingly one took it all in your stride and it was "business as usual" whilst on alert for an escapee. I actually did nurse prisoners from time to time and they were little different to the rest of the patients, with a sense of humour and generally respectful to us. I suppose many of them had just got in with the wrong crowd or had a moment of uncontrollable anger and then "too late" the crime is committed and the law has to take over. Yes, they must pay the price for what they have done but I always say "There but for the Grace of God go I" and am a firm believer in rehabilitation and preparation to re-define themselves and make something of their life on release. It is good to see a more positive approach to prisoner's rehabilitation in this century looking to creating transformation and empowerment. Of course there will always be those that choose not to change, some will re-offend because prison is their only "security" from being homeless and they probably feel powerless to change.

Nursing prisoners does somehow help you look much more objectively about the whole issue of crime and punishment. I am grateful for the experience.

Chapter 6

Tears and Laughter

The journey to finally receiving my State Registration Qualification was a combination of joy, fear and sadness as I continued to work on my self confidence. The hierocracy rules were strict and there were separate dining rooms for students and qualified Staff Nurses used the same Nurses Dining Room but you did not sit with anyone in a more Senior Position than you were. Sisters and Senior Administration Staff had their own Dining Room and I believe they had waitress service also. Food was made on the premises and was very basic but satisfied hunger after a busy shift. One got used to a lack of cutlery and many a time a knife handle or fork was used to stir ones tea or coffee due to a lack of teaspoons. Lift your cup for the final mouthfuls of coffee and in a blink, the saucer is whisked away plus plate as the final mouthful of food enters the mouth. Dining Room Staff want to get their work done in time or even early. The forks stirring strategy became a little engrained in my brain and one fateful day when at home on my off duty time, Mummy had forgotten to put a teaspoon on my cup and saucer – no mugs then and not in our house as Mother had spent many year in Domestic Service! Instinctively I picked up my knife and began stirring my tea, not thinking. "Don't you bring your filthy habits home here!" Mothers voice roared "Leave them at the hospital!" Oops!! Should have put brain into gear first! Needless to say I did not do it again. Neither did Mummy forget to put a teaspoon for me to stir with!.

Well back to the tears and laughter of Nurse Training in the 1960's. Before going onto the wards for practical experience there was more training to do with Nurse Tutor so we understood all the body systems of anatomy and physiology along with the procedures we would have to carry out on patients. Two particular incidents come to mind that caused amusement to my "set" as we were called.

It was time to learn how to pass a tube to the stomach for feeding patients who had conditions which meant that taking ordinary food was not suitable. To our horror, after preparing the equipment on a pristine clean trolley, Tutor picked up the tube known as Ryles Tube and began passing it up her nose, into her throat and swallowed it till it reached her stomach without as much as a "retch" or watering of the eyes!! Crumbs, I hope we don't have to do this I thought!!! Thankfully we did not have to indulge in what was a regular training ritual with her.

The other vivid memory is from our gynaecological teaching and training regarding the Female Reproductive System and Menstruation. On this day Tutor arrived complete with a copy of the Holy Bible – St James Version – which had passages highlighted in red in the books of the Old Testament. These were read out with great feeling as we were enlightened about Women's Menstruation through the ages! Bible reading for me would never be the same again!

We had many a moment of laughter over this particular lesson. Sometimes our training included lectures from eminent Professors in Medicine and Surgery. Some were superb in their expertise but not adept at putting it across in a classroom situation. Often designated to teach after lunch – the graveyard slot – it was all one could do to stay awake. The thought of exams on the subject somehow triggered closing eyes to struggle open and the hand to write notes. The writing helped greatly to prevent from "nodding off"

Once lecture that stays with me to this day is on diseases of the lungs when a beautifully presented pair of lungs in a jar was placed on the table in the front of the classroom, by the great Professor who then proceeded to write research statistics on the blackboard regarding the link between smoking and Lung Cancer. The lungs in the jar were jet black with lumpy white bits showing – cancer cells. Enough to put anyone off smoking! Ironically enough though many Doctors and Nurses did smoke to relieve stress levels. Even more bizarre was to hear a doctor telling a patient to give up smoking whilst smelling strongly of cigarettes themselves!

One of my first ward "experiences" was the Gynaecological Ward. The ward structure was very different to now with long rows of beds on either side with curtains to pull round the bed for "security" despite the fact that often a "discreet" chat with a Junior Doctor could be heard throughout the whole ward. Still the curtains gave both patient and doctor a sense of being in a totally soundproof room where no-one for miles around could hear. Known as Nightingale Wards – named after the famous Florence Nightingale who founded the modern day nursing, with key words and beds crammed in along each side – they did have some advantages. It was very easy to notice if a patient had obvious changes taking place such as breathing patterns or colour indicating something was going on internally and needed action. Bedmaking was always "up one side" and "down the other". Speed was key to getting the basic tasks done and we would set ourselves challenges to see who could make up an empty bed the fastest complete with mitred cornered sheets blankets and counterpane cover. The Top Sheet was turned over 18" and measured from elbows to fingers as a rough guide. On consultant round all patients had to be in bed sitting up if at all possible and bed linen pristine and not a crease in sight. Patients were jollily told "Don't move or breathe!"

Junior nurses were always a target for a "wind up" and the gynaecological ward was no exception. One day a first year nurse came onto the ward and the standard "wind up" routine took place. "Nurse will you go to the supplies store and tell them Sister has run out of fallopian tubes!!!" Not remembering in that moment that the fallopian tubes are actually part of the female anatomy the nurse duly goes to the supply store where they of course know the routine "What size does Sister require?" "She did not say" nurse replies nervously. "Go back and ask Sister which size she requires" he responds. Back to the ward goes Junior Nurse and quotes the supply officers request "he is asking what size you need Sister?" – "Oh tell him medium will be fine" Back goes Junior Nurse and tells the supplies officer what size Sister wants. "Sorry we are out of stock of medium size" Is the well rehearsed answer "Ask Sister to call me and discuss with us the order". Junior Nurse returns and relays the message and then Sister and staff in the office go into fits of laughter "Ever been had?" Thankfully Junior Nurse takes it in good spirits. No choice really! As a mere Senior Nurse on a joint training scheme I escaped the "Fallopian Tube" wind up routine!

Ward Sister was very strict with a Victorian approach to Management and we operated very much from a "fear of doing things wrong" mentality.

One morning during breakfast routine I stopped to empathise and mop up the tears of a lady at the bottom end of the ward. Within seconds a voice roared down the ward from Ward Sister (whose voice certainly made up for her height) "Nurse Bryden! What are you doing? Get on with serving breakfast!" No time for emotional support which saddened me but I had no choice but to get on with the routine. Sister must have grown up during the war years as she was a hoarder of coffee and sugar and there was always a good stack of it tucked away in the linen cupboard. In spite of the "Fear of God" put into us all we did learn a lot and the patients did get good practical care.

My time on the Medical Ward was very interesting being one of the "top six" London Hospitals. I was privileged to be part of the pioneering techniques of care and treatments. Each ward would have a single room which we called "The Side Ward" where patients needing one to one care resided. On Ward B4 Medical Ward I was able to be part of the very first concept of "Specialist Coronary Care" for patients who had suffered a heart attack, having to do one to one nursing with probably the first few patients to be treated in a totally new way that would enhance their overall recovery. It was common practice to see the first few patients in the main ward hooked up to heart monitors with the "beep beep" of their heart rate resonating throughout the ward. I felt proud to be a part of revolutionary medicine. Logging fluid intake was a major part of daily routine which the patients and I vividly remember. One of the weeks when it was my turn to make sure they were all up to date with "Ins" and "Outs" measured and ensuring all patients had partaken of sufficient fluids each day. If they were not accurately recorded the Consultant would have a few words to say as body fluid balance was all part of assessing how the patient was progressing. A big deficiency on the output side meant they were retaining fluid and further tests would be carried out. Well, this particular week, it was PM report time and Sylvia came on duty after her "two days off" to be greeted with "Nurse Bryden, why aren't these fluid charts up to date?" "I have been off duty for two days" I nervously replied "I don't care!" retorted Sister "You are responsible for the fluid charts! Get them up to date!" I did not dare argue but somehow managed to find out what I needed to know to sort the issue out. "Oh my!" I thought to myself "How on earth am I supposed to keep these up to date when I am not even on duty? Just grit your teeth and get on"

Sister would come to work on a bicycle come rain or shine and to keep warm, wore Royal Blue bloomers as part of her dress code for cycling. If they got wet in the heavy rain she would proudly hang them over the radiator in the office to dry! What a sight that was when you arrived for an early shift!!!! We nurses had many a laugh at her eccentric habit, I can tell you.

One of my most vivid training memories is being on a ward that was for patients having cancer treatment and also chronic pain. I was blessed to work with the Consultant who pioneered pain control and opened the first UK Hospice in Sydenham "St. Christopher's Hospice". She became a world renowned speaker and Knighted for her work with pain control - yes it was Dame Cicely Saunders in her pioneering days. I learned so much about the importance of creating a daily regime that kept patients pain free. The secret is to monitor pain levels, give appropriate drugs, doses and initially at exactly what time pain began to be felt again. The appropriate drugs would then be administered just before any pain kicked in and the regime then carefully monitored and pain relief drugs adjusted accordingly. The prescribed drug had to be administered at EXACTLY the right time and not a minute or less later. Woe betide any nurse that "forgot time" and the patient suffered unnecessary pain. If so you were in for a major dressing down from Dr. Cicely Sanders as she was then known. That experience impacted greatly on my nursing career and I would always do my very best to ensure that whatever it took, patients on pain relief had the same standard of care. It was very upsetting when at times, I would come across situations where GP's during my Community Nursing days were reluctant to assess and prescribe appropriate medication. Especially as the Dame Cecily Sanders approach to terminal care and chronic pain control actually worked!!! Only in rare situations such as bone cancer was pain relief regimes challenged. Working with patients going through terminal illness and chronic pain challenges made me aware of how blessed my life was with Health and Energy in spite of the food intolerance symptoms that I had suffered in my childhood.

It is good to reflect on our life regularly and see the blessings we do have and experience. Isn't each day a miracle in itself? A gift to our self to live it out the very best way we can with gratitude for even the smallest blessing or seeing the great lessons in our darkest hour.

I was very blessed to see things in my nursing years at a young age that truly made me aware of a greater force at work with us all, allowing experiences through physical form for the growth of our soul or higher self. Often people going through major challenges were the greatest teachers with their acceptance of the situation they were in and dignity to find humour in the midst of pain. "In every situation there is a hidden gift if we chose to acknowledge it".

Chapter 7

The Goal Achieved!

Time passes and before I knew it, I am in my final year of training with responsibility being placed on my shoulders to things such as junior nurse monitoring which enhanced all my practical skills along with knowledge. It was great to learn by experiencing "hands on" nursing during the training years. The discipline has been a great teacher for life generally. It creates greater self discipline in life and attention to detail. When someone's life is at risk and you are requested to do something there is no room for "I'll just finish this Sister!" A bit like the armed forces, there were times when if someone in authority said "jump" you did have to say "how high". I recall also the daily ward visit from the Senior Nurse Administrator who were answerable to Matron. They would be responsible for a certain number of wards and receive a report each day regarding all the patients on the ward.

It was a typical day on the gynaecological ward and Staff Nurse greeted the Nurse Administrator who did a ward round of all the patients while we dutifully continued our allocated tasks. Staff Nurse was a little "rusty" on the full diagnosis of each patient so decided to be creative. Understandably the women patients were in for either a Hysterectomy (removal of the uterus and ovaries) or a "D C" – scraping of the uterus or similar technique. So off she went with Admin Sister and proudly announced the reason for each patient as follows:-

"Hysterectomy, D & C, D & C, Hysterectomy, D & C, Hysterectomy" – repeatedly almost parrot fashion as she led her round the ward. Not only did they expect a correct diagnosis of all patients but their keen eye was also observing how clean the ward was and how fresh the flowers were etc. At the end of the ward round I heard her comment to Staff Nurse "Thank you Staff Nurse but I don't think you have that number of D & C patients do you? Oh and please see that the flowers on the windowsill are thrown away. We don't like dead flowers on display do we?" Oh my! She had done her homework from the ward report and knew about all the patients!! We did have a good laugh after she was gone and of course a junior nurse was duly requested to deal with the flowers and reprimanded for not noticing they were dead.

No stone was left unturned and it was very much like Wayne Dyers book "Excuses be gone!" even if your reason for anything missed was really quite valid!

My most "unfavourite" ward experience was a male medical chest ward where the patients would be coughing quite a lot due to chest infections and diseases. Each bedside locker would be adorned with an enamel "sputum mug" – basically a container with a handle and "flip-up" lid that contained a small amount of antiseptic liquid in the bottom, into which the patient would proudly deposit whatever they had coughed up. Each morning at around 10.00 a.m. a nurse would have to do the "sputum round" – yes it almost makes one gag writing this bit! All the sputum mugs were collected and each are observed and a note made on their appropriate chart as to the colour, texture, amount they had deposited. That was a task I truly did not like having to do.

It was on this ward that I recall we had a patient who had admitted from Wormwood Scrubs next door and would therefore have a Security Guard with him. One morning Security Guard had to go to relieve himself in the staff toilets and the patient took his chance – called a junior nurse to bring the telephone trolley, made a quick call and then he was gone. All hell broke loose when the security guard returned. Junior Nurse was duly reprimanded too! The hospital grounds were soon filled with Police and dogs hunting down the escapee. Never a dull moment during my training!

Now in my final year of training it was it was head down and start major revising for Hospital Final Exams and the State Registration exam to become a fully qualified General and Orthopaedic Nurse. Most free time was devoted to study and going over all that I had learned during my two and a half years at Hammersmith Hospital. Night Duty was sometimes a good time to revise if there were quiet spells.

Mostly times were interesting experiences. One of my allotted wards was a female cancer ward where radioactive "implants" were inserted to deal with Cervical and Uterine Cancer as part of the treatment regime. We all had to wear a special badge clipped to our uniform which were collected regularly and scanned with a Geiger counter machine to see if we had absorbed major amounts of radioactive materials. Junior Male Doctors would place their clip on badge as low down and in front of the body as possible believing it would "protect" their precious reproductive parts!!!

Once inserted into the woman's appropriate anatomy there was a strict timescale for the removal and placement into a special container for collection. Sometimes this would be in the middle of the night and needed great dexterity under a low light so as not to disturb the other patients. On one particular night with one patient, a colleague and I deftly prepared all that was required to remove the "object" from the patient. It was a spherical shaped metal radioactive cone with a chord that would be pulled out with special forceps and then the cone would pop out and be placed in the container. What happened next caused mayhem!!! Out popped the radioactive metal cone, left the forceps, and bounced down the ward and out of an open window onto some rubbish two floors below. We called up porters on duty and the next thing we saw out of the window are figures with torches and a Geiger counter searching for the offending object. We would have been told by Night Sister that we had been careless but in spite of it all she saw the humorous side of the situation. It made good reporting material when the day shift came on duty and of course the "Cone" was found and sent to the laboratory from whence it came originally.

Still frantically revising every possible moment away from my time on the wards the exams loomed nearer and nearer. We are given advice and guidance regarding how to write the exam paper and also the practical part of the examination. The practical part of the exam involved an oral exam where we had to answer questions about a typical scenario that might occur, role playing with patients plus setting up a few typical trolleys for procedures. At that time of my training we did not have procedure packs pre-prepared but had to be able to gather the necessary items and create the equipment of a modern day drug pack and type required, produce sterile pack and instruments to carry out a treatment.

I was shaking in my shoes when it came to the practical and oral Hospital Finals as I still had issues with dealing with authoritative people but somehow managed to control my fear and get through the exam and was amazed at how much knowledge I had retained and could recall. It was the same when the real exam day arrived which would determine whether I became a State Registered Nurse or not. I had no choice but to "face the fear and do it anyway" as the good book teaches us.

Imagine if Sylvia had allowed fear and past programming to be her master. There would have been no nursing career and who knows where her life would have taken her? Life is a journey of experiences and challenges to help us grow and learn how to fully express who we are – God manifesting and creating through physical form.

In May 1965 I recall gathering at a notice board and seeing whether I had passed the Hospital Final Exams. Hooray!!! I had received good marks and was well up on the leader board. With a sigh of relief I then continued to study for the State exams in June. In August the same year a letter arrived at my home and I insisted on opening it on my own with Mummy and Daddy out of the room. I felt sick in my stomach. Had I actually achieved my dream of qualifying as a nurse? My hands were shaking as I opened the envelope and tentatively unfolded the letter. Joy of Joys! My heart leapt as I read:-

> "Dear Miss Bryden
> We are pleased to announce that you have been accepted on the State Register of Nurses and can now apply for a uniform permit. Your State Registration Badge will be forwarded to you."

With tears running down my face I rushed out to tell my parents and they hugged me and showed how proud they were of me. Mummy had a few reservations I know as she also had really wanted to be a Nurse but was put into service instead.

Well here I am, August 1965, a fully qualified State Registered Nurse and Registered Orthopaedic Nurse. My determination and inner strength

The Goal Achieved!

from my spiritual self and "God's help" had got me over the hurdles and my dream becomes reality.

I can now legally practice my nursing skills at last. However, as with a goal achieved there is still more to learn and experience as the Sister on my current ward stated "Congratulations Nurse Bryden! Now you begin the real learning!"

Boy oh boy, how true that was!

I am to wear for the first time my Royal Blue Staff Nurses uniform and a different style of Nurses Cap. All nurses caps were a starched expertly folded crisp whitened cap that would be carefully kept in place by hair grips and complemented the smart look of the uniform dress, starched white apron and regulation highly polished shoes.

We will be presented our prizes and certificates by the Duke of Bedford – there is an attack of nervousness and what to say if he speaks to us when we go up on stage.

As I proudly accept my General Nursing and Orthopaedic Nursing Certificates and shake hands with the Duke of Bedford the visitors are clapping and I am sure there was a hint of a tear in my Mother's eyes. She would never normally show emotion so this was a moving moment. Refreshments are served and all relatives depart at the end of the afternoon.

Now I am fully responsible for my actions as a Registered Nurse. Excitement is coupled with some degree of trepidation at the thought of the decision making power I now have, as I begin the next phase of my journey having achieved a desire to become a nurse. However, the greatest feeling is that in spite of all the odds stacked against me I have achieved what everyone thought was impossible all those years ago. I have proved that "with God all things are possible", Vision, faith, determination and effort = Success.

If you have a dream or goal that burns deep within you – don't let it sleep through your life. Wake it up and do what it takes to fulfil it. Ignore those around you who would destroy your dream. Let your higher self lead and guide you. Face the fears and just "do it".

Chapter 8

Thrown in the Deep End

Well I had risen to the challenge of actually attaining my Nursing Qualification and knew that this was really the beginning of my "real learning" but did not expect to be so quickly thrown in at the deep end!

One week after my qualifying and returning to continue working on the ward for Arthritis and Pain Control, Ward Sister comes on duty and tells me that she is to go off on sick leave to have a hysterectomy and that I am to run the ward for the next three months at least! "You can do it" she said, "you took responsibility well in your final year of training and are very good at teaching the junior nurses as well. I have known you can do it and you have other Ward Sisters you can call on for support and advice"

What an accolade! My self esteem rose up through the fear and I felt an inner determination to make sure I lived up to Sister's expectations of me. Of course my inner spiritual self had faith in God and knew I would be guided and helped each day.

When I look back on this time I now see how this was the beginning of my being moulded for a greater purpose way down the line of my life journey. You see, life will guide us if we let it and do not always question "why me?" or "I can't do this!" Sometimes we have to jump in with both feet as we are led by our creative self, rather than allowing self pity that we will not draw in the experience, because our higher self knows what is best for a truly awesome journey on the earth plane. It is only the ego/programmed Mind that tries to destroy us. We can learn to override that and trust that "all is always in Divine Order". The more one connects with the inner "higher self" through prayer, meditation and love from the heart guidance – intuitive self – we will have a powerful and more joyous existence here on earth because we truly know that all things are possible. Consider that, with being "in the moment" instead of worrying what has happened or might happen, situations gradually unfold and become a moment by moment miracle experience of learning and growth.

Well, thankfully the ward and staff respected my way of leading them and running the ward, and even the Consultant's rounds went smoothly and I gained their respect too. The team and myself enjoyed a cup of coffee at the end of the round not only discussing patients but having a good laugh about something.

Consultant's "ward rounds" were a ritualistic affair and Ward Sister would sometimes get in a panic about them, getting nurses to sit patients upright in bed with all bedding neatly in order and nurses would rush around making sure everything was ultra pristine in appearance. This used to frustrate me as a student nurse because much as I respected Consultants I also believed that the patients care was a priority and that if the ward was a little chaotic when they arrived – so what? It would not interfere with the Consultant seeing the patient with his team of doctors. Thus it was, on Consultant Round days when I was running the ward were different. Especially if it was a morning event which was a busy time, washing patients and changing their beds as well as dressings to be done etc. Nurses would rush to me and say "It's Mr so and so's" round this morning isn't it? "Yes!" I would reply "Well the ward is not tidy and we still have patients to bed bath!" would be the panicky response. "So? The patients are our priority. The Consultant is doing his job just like the rest of us. He will take us as he finds us. Will it really make a great deal of difference?" I would retort. Ironically this was never an issue when I would tell the consultant the ward was a bit chaotic but the patients could still be seen. He would relax and we just got on with the task in hand. They would usually pull back bed clothes to examine patients and leave the bed in a mess anyway or take off a dressing to observe a wound or suture line and then it would need to be replaced. I actually found that the more relaxed approach seemed to be enjoyed by the Consultant and team.

I stayed on the same ward for almost a year gaining a good knowledge and experience and things seemed to run smoothly most of the time and we were a happy bunch of nurses caring for our patients until one day the cool, calm, efficient Sylvia lost her temper with a nurse. This was to be the first of about five times in my life where I really "blew my top" verbally in front of others. One of the student nurses had been assigned a task and repeatedly ignored my request to carry it out which meant that certain important information regarding patient care was not recorded over a period of days. On this particular day, as was seen, she seemed to be doing very little when it was really busy. Sylvia roared at her in front of the nurses and patients "Nurse will you please do what I have asked you to do several times, I am fed up with having to keep on at you about this. Just get on and do it NOW! I will not tolerate poor standards on this ward!" Well the ward came to a deadly silence. Here was happy, calm Staff Nurse Bryden behaving totally out of character. The nurse I had shouted at in public, sheepishly got on with her task and then I called her to the office and apologised for shouting in front of everyone but also reminded her of the importance of being responsible and carrying out tasks allocated to her. I also had the grace to apologise to the staff and patients and at report time used it as a teaching tool about how not to deal with a staff issue!

Time passed and eventually Ward Sister returned and I was relieved to hear that she was pleased with the how the ward had been managed in her absence. I had learned a great deal during that time. It was a good grounding for my future times yet to unfold.

It was considered good nursing practice to do ones midwifery training soon after qualifying and so Sylvia applied for the one year training and was successfully accepted to take the first part of midwifery training at the hospital in Woolwich that was linked to the Salvation Army.

Here we are with a new challenge - to deal with new lives coming into the world. I enjoyed my 6 months and delivered some babies under supervision, my proudest moment being when I helped a Mother successfully deliver a 10lb (4.5Kg) baby without having to do an episiotomy cut or her having a tear. I still have a photograph of the baby in my possession as a keep - sake.

Part of the training involved a time on night duty shifts. This was a challenging time, with 30 babies in a nursery whilst mothers slept and all needed night feeds. With only two nurses on duty it took some doing I can tell you! Especially if a number of the babies awoke at the same time for a feed. A very warped sense of humour kept us calm as my colleague would say "Ok! Whose first out of the window!" Of course we would not have harmed any of those dear little souls.

They all had their own individual personalities. There was, however, one baby with real copper coloured hair and a strong personality whereby it cried incessantly and was never satisfied having been fed, winded and changed. Night Sister gave us permission to segregate the baby to the bathroom for the night. I am sure it was the "perfect" baby during the day just eating and sleeping, happy to be near its mother! Sometimes I have wondered whether shutting the baby in the bathroom – even with regular checks – had a psychological effect on it as it grew into adulthood!

My best memory of this period is Mother's Day on the ward. In the morning we would take the babies out of the nursery and give them to their mother for the morning feed and cots stayed by the bed for the daytime. On Mother's Day we put a tiny posy of African Violets in the hand of each baby before taking them out to greet their mothers. The response was very emotional as Mothers and Nurses had tears in their eyes. It was a very moving sight. The African Violet is said to mean Romantic Love. Giving birth to one's baby will of course manifest deep feelings of love!

Successful at the first part of Midwifery Training, I travelled to Kent for my Part II training in Dartford and enjoyed 6 months alongside a typical Community Midwife of many years experience with a broad Irish accent who knew all the local gossip and kept the mothers entertained with stories and anecdotes during their labour and they were so relaxed and having a good laugh that very little medication was needed to relax them during the contractions. Deliveries took place in varied states of cleanliness and despite poor conditions we could create a clean area in some very interesting home environments.

I recall delivering a baby in a downstairs basement flat which had little or no heating – wouldn't be allowed now! Rather grey coloured bedding was pulled back and mother placed on what we hoped were clean towels ready for delivering her baby. Husband was present for the whole delivery time and we did our best not to feel cold as the flat was not only limited with lighting but also suffering with dampness! After some time baby's head appears and then out we pop. The room temperature not being ideal, steam rose from the baby as it uttered it's first cry! Hastily we wrap it in towels and cut the umbilical chord. Placenta is successfully delivered and the baby checked over and weighed on portable hanging scales. A good average weight of around 7lbs 8oz (3.5Kg). On our return later in the day mother and baby are doing well and baby really did thrive in spite of the environment! Probably made it a "tough cookie" with a strong immune system and resilient as it grew up!

Not knowing when a baby would decide to come into the world meant we were on call at night as well. One evening I had just washed my hair and had rollers in to give it a curl, when the phone rang – "Mrs......... is in labour, I will pick you up now" What would I do? I had to put a scarf over my rollers and get into uniform and I spent the night with my hair drying whilst assisting the midwife and mother. Baby was delivered around 6 a.m. and I was allowed to go home and rest for a little while before continuing the assigned duties for the rest of the day alongside a midwife who never seemed to get tired – just got on with the job she so loved!

I enjoyed my time in the community and felt that deliveries were a lot less stressful in the home environment. If there were any challenges, a Doctor was on call, plus an ambulance could come and take the mother quickly to hospital. This seemed to be a very rare occurrence.

Again I was successful with Part II exams and was now proud of my achievement of General Nursing, Orthopaedic Nursing plus Midwifery success. A long way from the sickly, nervous and extremely shy little girl not expected to succeed!

Sylvia's confidence was growing more and more and life was much more fun. I was attending church again in Dartford, as I stayed with friends mostly whilst off duty, and it was time for another "in at the deep end" experience. Deep inside I still had a nagging insecurity and often experienced "butterflies as big as elephants" but learned to override them and become used to living a life of outward confidence and inner fear. The inner fear of course made one very sensitive to any criticism and fear of authority resulting in being a total "Yes" person when the word "No" should have been in my vocabulary. The one area I did have the courage to say no, was with a boyfriend who became my fiancé. He was a member of the church I was going to and also the brother of the husband where I was staying. We became very close and he asked me to marry him. During that time I was experiencing real affection and I said

"Yes". However, after a period of time I suddenly realised that I could not bear the thought of waking up with him in bed every morning so told him I had changed my mind and gave him my engagement ring back. He subsequently met someone else, married and she became the dutiful Pastor's wife – not my idea of a good marriage. No-one was ever going to control Sylvia anymore!!!

CHAPTER 9

The Winding Road of Experience Begins

Having established a career foundation it was time for Sylvia to begin to spread her wings – especially now she was "free" from ever being "trapped" in a marriage that would have created a boxed in life whereby the inner free spirit would have created a purpose not yet realised and would not have been able to express itself fully.

Looking back over my life and the incredible journey I have followed, brings a realisation of how what we can consider to be challenges and inner sufferings are but experiences our soul chooses, to develop our skills to help humanity.

Somehow my career path was once again bringing opportunities.

Although I had enjoyed my Midwifery training it was not my burning desire to stay in this field of nursing. Something within me wanted to experience more. I decided to return to my Orthopaedic Nursing which I had so loved and applied for a Night Superintendent's Post at the London Branch of the Royal National Orthopaedic Hospital in Great Portland Street. I was successful and enjoyed nearly 2 years running the hospital overnight. Sleeping during the day was a challenge. I was "living in" on the premises with a room overlooking Great Portland Street and the underground station – a very busy street with traffic going all day long. Even taking a sleeping tablet was useless. I decided that relaxing and getting 3 hours quality sleep was preferable to the feelings created by the sleeping tablets.

My food intolerance still affected me from time to time with headaches and intestinal cramps plus typical "Irritable Bowel" type symptoms. One evening whilst preparing for the night shift, I began to get mega cramps in my abdomen and thought I was heading for Appendicitis and possibly hospital admission. Determined to work that night I packed a bag with basic overnight kit and reported for duty saying nothing to anyone. I completed the first evening ward rounds and was visited in the office by one of the staff nurses who had noticed I looked pale and unwell. "Are you alright Sister" she asked with kindness and concern. I related my story and it was suggested that I rest for a few hours and would be called if needed as the hospital was "quiet" with nothing major going on. The rest and a warm drink seemed to calm my guts and by morning I was fine with no sign of my "self diagnosis". The overnight bag was returned to my room and unpacked with a great sigh of relief!

Now in my mid twenties and still single I threw myself into my career as opposed to being desperate for marriage. Somehow the strict childhood and lack of confidence around relationships prevented me from being successful in finding a partner. I was still fairly happy with my lot and held onto my spiritual faith as my "crutch" for life.

My next venture in the nursing world was yet again indulging in Night Duty experience in a hospital in New Cross, London. This was a general hospital with more emphasis on medical care and spread over a large area of land. This meant rather "spooky" walks to get to the wards and climbing low lit stairs up to many of the wards. There was little security apart from the two Porters who spent the night in their comfy little den – the Porters Lodge - in between walking the grounds at night to look for any predators who might be lurking. They were also responsible for taking the bodies of patients who died to the mortuary and as this was an old hospital without lifts it meant carrying a trolley up to the ward and then down the stairs again complete with the body inside. One night Sylvia was doing her usual 2 a.m. ward round when she caught sight of the two night porters armed with bright torches grovelling around in the bushes at the bottom of the stairway to one of the wards. "What are you doing?" I asked "Well it's like this Sister" replied one of them "you see, the trolley caught on the bottom stairs" says the other "and then the lid opened and the body shot out and its somewhere in the bushes!!!!" "We'll find it Sister, its OK". Trying not to laugh and be respectful to the deceased, I continued on my way to the ward to check that all was well. I did go and see the Porters in their snug little lodge later and have a cup of tea and ensure that the body was fully intact and safely in the Mortuary.

It is early evening round time on one rather fateful night and I enter the ward to see a group of ladies playing with a "ouija" board to call up the spirits of the departed. I was horrified. My strict Pentecostal Church upbringing did not approve of such things – it was the work of the Devil!!! "What's going on here?" I asked very angrily standing to my full height of 5ft 2 ½ inches (156.25 cm) in modern terms. "Oh!" says one of the ladies "We do this every evening to try to get my husband to come through and talk to us! "Well not when I am on duty" I retorted. "We do not want any evil spirits coming here thank you – you do not know what you might attract playing with that – now put it out of my sight now please!" Sheepishly they gathered everything together and put the board safely in a cupboard. Interestingly my views and beliefs have broadened greatly since that time and I am blessed to channel messages for those grieving loved ones in a protected and safe way bringing along messages from God's world to help people. However, I must say her that I still do not personally approve of the 'ouija' board method of communication. Apart from the two memorable events, the nights went quite smoothly and during the night when I was not called for major emergencies I would sit in my office and click away with my knitting needles for friends, children and myself – Cable, FairIsle patterns as well as good old knit one pearl one stitches. Mummy taught me how to knit and did an excellent job.

I had had at least two and a half years of night duty experience and it was taking a toll on my physical body. Adjusting to sleeping in the daytime for most of the week – four nights on and three nights off – and often tired at night time made me almost permanently tired, so I decided it was time for a change.

One morning I was taking the air, before going to bed to rest and walked past the British School of Motoring Driving School in Peckham High Street. Something within seemed to take me inside and before I could even fully rationalise my action I had booked a series of driving lessons. Never having possessed a bicycle, I had little road sense except "Jay walking" in between cars across Oxford Street during my training days at the Hammersmith Hospital. Later that day it suddenly dawned on me what I had done. "Oh well here's to the challenge Sylvia!" was my inner response. My driving instructor was a woman who was far from calm in her make up and took me around all the quiet streets of Peckham most of the time until one day it was considered to be alright for me to be let loose around the busier streets of the Peckham area. I recall vividly the lessons which made me more nervous as each time "Mind that Bus!" she would cry "I've been under a bus once this week already!" My confidence really was increased – or not- by such statements. After 10 lessons I decided to take some more instruction in the Dartford area where I was staying with friends on my off duty times. This time I had an independent ex - police driving instructor who managed to get me up to the required standard and successful in passing my driving test first time of application. The first lesson was very interesting. He took me through the town and around one ways systems and then out onto a dual carriageway heading south from Dartford. "More gas! More gas!" I kept hearing in my ears "This is a 40 mph speed limit!" Panic set in as with the B.S.M. Instructor I had barely exceeded 25 mph around Peckham. Then, horror of horrors, we are approaching a major roundabout "I've never driven round a roundabout" nervously came from my lips "Well you are about to do it right now!" was his response. Somehow I managed to negotiate the roundabout successfully and continue on the dual carriageway. "Take the next left turn please" he instructed "and then do a first right turning". We were in a rather desolate car parking area and I pulled in and parked up as requested. "I think we had better go back to the beginning and start again" he calmly but firmly stated "I have never rated the BSM that highly. How many lessons did you have with them?" "10" I replied with many moths and butterflies in my tummy. "A bit of a waste of your time and money. I'll get you through your test if you do what I say and you must practice in between lessons as well!" Now let's get you home." I drove the car back to home feeling rather sad and wondering if I was doing the right thing – should I continue or give up? Determination and inner courage rose from somewhere and decided to continue. My own car was now required and that was a bit of a ironical challenge against my salary, but with the help of good friends, I found a black 1949 split windscreen Morris Minor that I hand painted to improve its looks and cover any small rust spots we treated. Husband would take me out for practice and I seemed to be doing well. Reversing round corners was an interesting lesson. I ended up over the curbs initially with cries from the instructor of "Get that car off the grass verge!" "I don't want people seeing that – it will give a bad impression!" Almost in tears, my confidence was crushed by the authoritarian tones. Yet still I persevered. "I Will do it" I thought through the emotions. "It will not get the better of me!" The Test day arrived and I felt more nervous than the day I took my Nursing Final Examination. The examiner shouted at me for staying in 3rd gear too long at one point and my inner reaction was "That's it I've failed. What the heck!" With some anger at his manner, continued to drive, plus more assertively. Amazingly I passed first time. My first experience on the road on my own was the drive to New Cross Hospital that very evening – in at the deep end! I successfully negotiated the busy traffic and New Cross one way system. Gave a huge sigh of relief on reaching the hospital. The Head Nurse of Day Duty came to hand over to me for the night "Gosh! – You look like you've seen a ghost! Are you alright!" "I've just driven here after passing my test" I replied. "Oh Ok – thought you were ill or something! Glad you got here safely" A few of the ward nurses would pop in during the night to see me about something and I was apparently still looking rather pale. By then the pallor had nothing to do with my journey into work. My reply to their comments about my lack of colour would be. "I've passed my driving test and drove here last night. I am petrified of the drive home in the rush hour traffic!" However, I did get safely back home and fell into bed for a hopefully "good days sleep"

I was becoming a good example of the book by "Face the Fear and do it Anyway" which I was later to read as it was not yet published.

A little advice to my readers – if you want to do something in life – DO IT!!!! Don't let fear stop you. If you make a mistake, learn from it, and keep on keeping on. After all, life is a journey of wonderful experiences if we could but see it thus.

Chapter 10

Health – the Challenge re-emerges!

My challenges with my health during childhood did settle somewhat during my teens and my physical body somehow was coping with the intake of wheat and dairy products. However, I still did have some throat and sinus problems pop up fairly regularly for which I took antiseptic lozenges and "over the counter" purchase items until:- I had been working during my third year of Nurse Training. I became victim of tonsillitis and kept on working and sucking lozenges. The pain and discomfort got increasingly worse and after three weeks of putting up with symptoms I nearly collapsed whilst on duty. A visit to the hospital doctor available for staff to see was immediately actioned and I was apparently working with a very high temperature, tonsils full of infection and very swollen. Against my wishes I was ordered to sick bay to rest and have emergency antibiotic treatment. This entailed being given antibiotic injections into my buttocks initially for 5 days. Sylvia was now about to experience what she had regularly administered to patients - "the other side of the fence" encounter. I decided that I would show how injections of thick fluid into muscle was not as painful as many patients declared was the case. Well! Was I in for a surprise!!! After my first injection I felt the need to go to the toilet and put on my dressing gown, stepped out of bed and started to walk towards the toilets. Indescribable pain shot down my right leg through the Sciatic Nerve and I had to immediately stop my journey for a second, continuing to hobble to the toilet! A big lesson learned here. I had heard many nurses say to patients who had injections of viscose liquids for various treatments "Come now! Don't make such a fuss!" Never again would Sylvia ever think of a patient not being able to deal with pain. I had quite a high pain threshold and still felt the agony of the injection.

It is all too easy to judge others against our own standards when we are all so different and experiencing our own journey of life. Thankfully as the years went on pain control and pain level monitoring were an important part of assessment. Patients with low pain thresholds were treated accordingly rather than mocked at as "making a fuss". I had been advised to rest a while before getting out of bed. However, Sylvia's "I'm OK" tendency and "I'll show them it's only an injection" mentality took over and having given into the major infection and obeying instructions to rest I soon realised that actually I did need rest. Even that seemed a challenge.

Concerned for my welfare, friends and colleagues came visiting – after night duty, end of a shift and during the "split duty" free time in the afternoon. So all day long somebody was rushing in to visit. I hadn't got the heart to say "Go Away I want to sleep now!" So I dutifully made myself stay awake – with difficulty at times. Why weren't Sick Bay visiting times restricted like the other wards? Still, if Sylvia had asserted herself she would have got her times of rest. The word "No" was far away from my vocabulary then. In fact it did not even exist. It was many years later that I became comfortable with saying "NO", having realised that we are as important to nurture as well as others. If we tell others that they need to have their "ME TIME" then, excuse me, would it not be a good idea to lead by example? Oh dear! How programmed we become!

In spite of being overly bombarded with visitors I was allowed out of sick bay after around 10 days and then a couple of days home with my parents before returning to my duties.

During my stay in Sick Bay my intuitive skills came into play, albeit I was unaware of the gift I had deep down. One afternoon a friend of mine who was working on the ward adjacent to the Sick Bay came over for 5 minutes tea break. "It's manic over there" she cried "Can't you get out of bed and help?" We laughed "Mrs Suchabody is very ill and looks as if she isn't long for this world. Could do without that amongst everything else that is going on!" Jokingly I said "Oh I expect she will go around 6.00 p.m.

just as you're about to serve supper!" Well at two minutes past 6 a figure rushed into Sick Bay and cried "I wish you would keep your mouth shut!! She went at exactly 6.00 o clock!" "Sorry" I responded sheepishly knowing that she was not angry just annoyed that I had "predicted" absolutely accurately. I was rather curious myself too.

I remained in relatively good health with angry sinus problems and occasional sore throats and was used to regular "bowel releases" as my body desperately tried to deal with the toxins I was building up. I had another major intolerance reaction – albeit I was unaware what it was a few years later when I suddenly developed severe abdominal pain – more than the bloating and "wind" I regularly had – and developed severe diarrhoea resulting in Sylvia having sick leave for three weeks. I survived on cream crackers and marmite for nearly three weeks and became very weak. To drink tea made me extremely nauseous and I was beginning to think I would never enjoy a cup of good old English tea again! Not being able to indulge in my usual high dairy and wheat diet which included jam donuts, iced buns, chocolate éclairs filled with cream was probably allowing a major detox to occur. Living in the toilet nearly all day and night initially was my routine. Once over the episode I, of course, returned to my standard diet filling my body with foods it really could not tolerate. It is amazing how resilient our human bodies are but of course they will react and "complain" if we treat them badly and abuse with the wrong support for health and wellness. My perception of me was that I was healthy and had good energy in spite of regularly having these symptoms and sometimes rolling around the floor with chronic "wind". After I had eaten I would feel a pulsation in my abdomen which I had experienced since childhood and it became part of my body's "norm". The next health challenge – again food related of which I was ignorant – was regular migraine headaches that left me fully exhausted for at least 3 – 4 days. These occurred at around three weekly intervals. I still figured I was a healthy and fit individual and continued my wheat and dairy diet by now indulging also in clotted cream teas whilst on holiday! Alcohol was also on the social agenda during my "freedom years" enjoying schooners of sherry or three, Bacardi and Coke or Martini and Lemonade. Very seldom did I have a hangover except one fateful night staying in a caravan with a group of friends and Sylvia mixed the types of sherry. What an interesting night that was! By bedtime – at least 2.00

a.m. in the morning – I was talking for England and could not shut up. Banished to the far end of the caravan to sleep on the narrow sofa I spent all night **shouting** with a repetitive cry of "I do feel sick, oh I do feel sick, but I'm never sick" as the caravan swayed around me. Eventually I must have dropped off into an alcoholic sleep and somehow managed a full English breakfast on rising. Friends teased me all day. Thankfully they had a great sense of humour and had their own "morning after" symptoms to deal with. The rest of the holiday was spent with great frivolity where alcohol was concerned! My alcohol intake reduced as well and the Martini and Lemonade replaced the sherry with far less "side effects". No! Cigarettes never became part of my unhealthy regime. It wasn't so much the religious discipline as the experience at the age of ten years that impacted. Daddy, having been in the Royal Navy for around 20 years was a smoker and indulged in good old strong Players or Woodbine cigarettes and the butt ends were usually adorning ash trays around the home ready for Mummy to clear away. One day curiosity got the better of me "Hmmm I thought to myself – if Daddy smokes cigarettes, it must be nice" (I had great love and respect for him) So what did I do? Picked up a butt end from one of the ash trays and started to chew on it. I rushed to the toilet and spat it out down the toilet pan and nearly "threw up". I cannot describe the taste in my mouth but I vowed there and then cigarettes would NEVER be in my life again. Bless you Daddy for your butt ends! My non smoking was sealed when an eminent Professor gave a lecture in 1965 about research that had been carried out over the last 20 years that proved conclusively that smoking was related to lung cancer. The black lungs full of tar that he dissected in front of us re-enforced the statistics also. Not everyone was affected by his vividly illustrated lecture as many of my nursing colleagues were already addicted to the habit and had the attitude "Well not everyone gets Cancer" or "Well my Grandad/Grandma smoked and lived till their 90's" That was their choice and what the consequences were for them health wise I never found out. I am ever grateful for my choice on this issue. Life is all about choices albeit often excuses are made rather than accepting that we are all empowered with the gift of free will and can choose what we wish to experience throughout this earthly journey. Sylvia's choices of food and alcohol would have been very different if knowledge of food intolerances was known during her earlier years!

Chapter 11

Twists and Turns in my Nursing Career

By 1971 I was ready for yet another challenge and applied to be a District Nurse (Community Nurse as the title is now) and began working in the Greenwich Health Authority. Strict uniform again with Royal Blue dresses, Navy Blue Blazer or winter coat and a brushed velour hat to be worn throughout all seasons, plus of course, good old Clarks regulation shoes that were well polished. A standard "kit" was given us in a leather bag, just like you see on the old TV Programmes. After two weeks induction, I am given my own "round" consisting of around 40 patients who lived in the Woolwich and Plumstead Areas.

A map book is given to me to help me find my way around the given route. Here we go again! I have a list of up to 18 patients to see on a given day varying from assisting them to wash and dress, wound dressings and injections and guess what? Sylvia does not know how to read a map!! "OK I thought" If I am to do this work I have to learn to map read. Giving myself a maximum of 28 days to master map reading, I set off on day one, turning the pages upside down, on their side trying to get the hang of left turning, right turns and general directions, my brain hurt by the end of the first day. Thankfully some of the patients were in adjoining streets which did help somewhat.

The map reading challenge was overcome during the 28 days deadline and I was soon able to "reverse" read the pages and find my way – determined as always!

By now my car choice had changed to a Ford Saloon and I was purchasing it via a local authority loan at very low interest rates. It felt good to have a brand new car to drive around in. Very quickly my car and I became well known to the local Police. No – not for offences but locking myself out with the keys inside! Back then it was possible to push down the button in the inside of the door, hold the door opening handle upwards, shut the door and it was instantly locked. Very easy when one's rushing around to get 18 patients done in a day. That is how I managed to lock myself out and I had many a visit from the local "Bobby's" with their master keys. The other method – if the windows were open a little way, was to bend a metal coat hanger in such a way that it would hook around the locking button inside and lift it up. Yes! You have guessed! I always had a metal coat hanger with me or requested one from the patient.

Once a week I travelled to Croydon College to learn the theory relating to working in the community and after one year successfully passed the National District Nursing Examination. Sylvia was now eligible to have more responsibility and therefore became even more accountable for her actions as a District Nurse. I loved my time in this field of nursing, building great respect with patients and their families. Many of the houses I visited were pre-war dwellings without hot water and one house had gas lamps on the walls which were still in use. Outside toilets were commonplace in some of the Plumstead houses and I had to sometimes indulge in the unpleasant experience of sitting on a wooden box with a hole in it as I was desperate for the loo. They did at least have a cistern that flushed and then thankfully there were no spiders lurking!!!

In my early District Nursing years, Sterile Dressing Packs did not exist and we would boil instruments on the patient's cooker and sterile the components by baking in the oven in a red biscuit tin – the patients or family would bake the tin prior to our visit so that we had a sterile gauze and swabs to use. Hands would be thoroughly washed and forceps used for the whole procedure. There were no disposable gloves available either. Diabetic patients had their own glass syringes which they kept in sterile fluid and the insulin dose had to be calculated. No convenient injection pens. Mental arithmetic was an essential part of the nursing kit.

Patients grew attached to their nurse and would get upset if suddenly they disappeared. Sometimes, Management would review the geographics of the areas we were allocated and change things which meant that we had some of our "regulars" taken from us and others given to us to care for. Day one of this change was always very interesting. With bated breath one entered the homes of the new patients who had been privileged to have the same nurse for months or even years. "Where's my nurse?" was the cry "I want my nurse!" Explanations were diplomatically given and gradually rapport was built. Some were so incensed about the changes, they contacted our headquarters and made a formal complaint. Not that it did much good - the usual response would be "I am sure you will find Nurse ***** as friendly and caring as your other nurse". Occasionally when covering the area of some of the patients transferred, they would welcome you almost with open arms. "Have missed you – how are you?" In this work you almost became one of the family and the trusted confidant as they poured out their troubles and family problems to you. If there was time it was good manners to accept a cup of tea or coffee after completing the required task.

Talking of cups of tea and coffee reminds me of one particular lady who had a monthly visit for an injection of Vitamin B12 – typical treatment for Pernicious Anaemia. She lived alone and my visits were very welcome as she seldom got out and had no family nearby. After the first visit I did almost dread the future ones and here is why. "You must have a cup of coffee Nurse! Oh, and I have some nice fruit cake for you as well. I am sure you can manage a piece to keep you going!" "Thank you very much, that's very kind of you" I responded and dutifully sat at the dining room table with its heavy duty velour table cover on. Off she went through the scullery to a tiny kitchen with a gas cooker – one of the original post war designs – table, Belfast Sink with wooden draining board and a cold water tap. Eventually she appears with a cup of milky coffee in one hand and a plate with a chunky sized piece of fruit cake on the other. I love fruit cake, so was looking forward to an indulgence served with great kindness. I took a bite and tried very hard not to show my horror – it was very stale! "How long has this been in the cupboard?" I thought as I politely say "It's lovely. Thank you very much!" She sat talking as I ate the cake whilst wondering how my stomach would react. There was nowhere or no way I could sneak it into a pocket or nursing bag. It was like she was determined that Nurse would enjoy the cake. Relieved at the last mouthful I swallowed I relished the idea of at least washing it down with the coffee. Oh dear! Guess what? As Sylvia drank the first mouthful it was very obvious that this lady had memory problems – yes, you have guessed – the milk was very sour and well out of it's "drink by date" With my stomach almost heaving, I finished the coffee out of politeness, booked her in for the next visit and left. The gutter looked almost inviting to throw up the contents of my stomach but somehow I managed to keep it down and drove to the next patient. The ritual was repeated monthly for over a year until I changed the area I worked. Best of luck to the next victim!!! were my thoughts, along with relief that the experience was over. Oh yes, I recall one other visit with this lady where she produced a jar of homemade jam for me to take with me. "This may be alright" I thought as I accepted another gift of gratitude. When I reached home later, I decided to inspect the contents of the carefully labelled and prepared jar of jam. Tentatively I removed the red gingham cover and elastic band followed by the wax disc covering the jam only to find a thick layer of green "penicillin" that had grown! Of course I had to tell a lie on the next visit when asked if I had enjoyed the jam, I let her believe that I certainly had. Of course the intent was one of gratitude for the help and company that she enjoyed on each visit. I did not have the heart to tell her how awful and stale everything was, as she was giving from the heart.

Isn't it important to focus on the intent behind gifts in the life rather than the gift itself? This is superbly illustrated by another patient I used to visit daily. She lived alone and was not very mobile due to ulcerated legs, plus she was blind. Every day she went to her blind club and would do knitting – something she enjoyed. It was Christmas Day and I was working during the morning and called on this lady to do her leg dressings. "Happy Christmas" I called out as I entered "Happy Christmas Nurse" she echoed with a smile. Dressings completed, she fumbled in a box near her chair and pulled out a little parcel. "This is for you nurse for all your help and kindness" "I will open it when I get home. Thank you so much – really you should not have!!" was my reply with emotions rising within. Later at home with friends, I opened her gift after all the others I had been given. Tears came to my eyes as I pulled out a knitted cotton dishcloth. Some would say it was only a common old dishcloth but I knew she had made this with love and gratitude. As I write this to you I still feel emotional.

The gift meant more to me than all the other gifts I had been given. There was a moment of silence when I opened it, as all around me were learning something about the intent of a gift rather than the size and price of a gift.

My Community Nursing years taught me much about the dynamics of disease being cared for at home. Pressure on families trying to juggle their own life and care for a loved one or neighbour. Decisions regarding care at home or 24 hour nursing home care. Helping patients to be able to stay in their own homes for as long as possible. In amongst the dynamics were joyous times when one witnessed recovery of the surgery and remissions following cancer treatments.

Probably the most rewarding and emotionally moving part of community care is nursing terminal illness in the home. One almost becomes part of the family over a period of time. The journey of denial through to acceptance with patient and family is a great teacher about dealing with one's own life situations. One particular patient I nursed was a confirmed Atheist and had been all her life. The last few days of her life here on earth were to be very inspiring. Heading in and out of consciousness she seemed to become very calm and serene with total absence of fear of dying. About 48 hours before she passed, when I did one of my many visits, she opened her eyes, smiled and with great calmness and with conviction stated "Nurse, I am not afraid to die. I have been there and seen it. It is so beautiful". As she spoke there was a light that seemed to emanate from her eyes and a sense of peace that filled the bedroom. The next day she passed over and I was able to comfort the family with her words. How can we deny another existence after we leave our physical body when one witnesses such an experience? Attending funerals of patients one had nursed for a considerable period of time and then passed into the world of "God" or "Spirit" was accepted practice. Dressed in smart uniform one would turn up at the crematorium or cemetery chapel for the service. Often this was an emotional experience bringing back memories of the funerals of one's own loved ones now in a happier place. Usually, it was possible to slip away back to duties at the end of the service. However, I recall one occasion when I was ready to slip away and was accosted by a key family member who introduced me to distant relatives who had "Come out of the woodwork" at the time of near passing of the patient. A voice then quietly, but firmly – out of the earshot of the relatives – said to me "You will come back to the house Nurse – won't you?" "Well I really should get back to my duties" I replied. "Nurse, please, please come for a short while! You see, so and so are here and after a drink all hell will be let loose about inheritance etc. I do not want rows at this difficult time." My kind heart overrode my duties", knowing I would just work a little later and back to the house I went. Crammed full of relatives and friends, I drank tea, ate sandwiches and made polite conversation about how I had really bonded with patient and family and witnessed a peaceful passing. The atmosphere seemed to be relatively calm and I was thanked for my presence as I left. When I returned for a bereavement visit a few weeks later, it was reported to me that my presence had dissipated any friction and arguments. It certainly made me feel happy about the decision I had made. The whole situation taught me a great deal about family dynamics at such sensitive times and the importance of family counselling before the patient passes so that things can be put in place to help prevent a family crisis occurring when someone is on the terminal illness journey.

My District Nursing Career was a very rewarding time and led me to working as a Specialist Nurse in the Cancer Care Arena working with Bowel Cancer Patients and Breast Cancer Patients. Helping people adjust to body image change was both challenging and rewarding. One saw couples become closer together through the journey and others gradually drift apart as the patients partner could not come to terms with the outcome of Bowel Cancer Surgery or Radical Mastectomy. How grateful I became for my health, although symptoms I was having due to food intolerances did at one point make me fearful of having bowel cancer and I was seriously considering which I could best live with – a Mastectomy or a Colostomy Bag! The Power of the Mind! It can so easily generate thoughts that definitely do not serve us.

I enjoyed the work and also learned much about how to create empathy with people from all walks of life and be totally non-judgemental and come from a centre of unconditional love.

This was a time in my life when I was beginning to work with alternative approaches to symptoms and looking at the influence of diet on health. Natural approaches to cancer were becoming more popular with a centre in Bristol, pioneering a revolutionary diet and meditative approach to cancer.

I recall one patient who had been treated for breast cancer and it was spreading. The Consultant sent her home with a six week life span. On my first home visit I found her in bed, head under the covers in a very depressive state. Here was a lovely lady who had a granddaughter that she adored and would help out at her school reading with children daily. It was around the month of June this visit took place. I decided to challenge her and told her of the power of incorporating natural approaches to her cancer. I also asked her if she wished to stay depressed and fade away or get up and fight the cancer – did she want more time with her granddaughter whom she so adored? Suddenly her whole body language and expression changed. "I'll fight this!" she said with determination as she sat up in bed "Where do we start?" We discussed her diet and supplements that would not compromise her other medication and her GP was in agreement. By the next day she had begun her new regime and by September she was back at school reading on a daily basis! Her life span was another three and a half years!!!

It was the initial change of mind set that triggered this lady's determination to get up and work at beating the cancer. There are many recorded cases of patients totally ignoring the doctor's declaration on their life span and going on to live many years. Our minds are very powerful and they can either disempower us or empower us. We have to be open to choose whether to believe what those around tell us or listen to our inner guide and follow that. We can allow our circumstances to control us or we can decide to be in control of our circumstances – take responsibility for our life journey and find ways to overcome obstacles.

After 5 years in the Cancer Counselling niche I was emotionally drained and fully ready for another experience but was not sure which way to go..... A Newspaper Advertisement was to change my direction quite dramatically.

PART 3

Another Twist to The Journey

Chapter 1

A Leap of Faith!!

One Summer's day as I was musing which way to take my career a dear friend of mine, whilst browsing the local paper, suddenly called out "Here Sylvia! Here's a job for you in the local paper!" "Don't be silly" I retorted "You **are** joking aren't you?" "Come and look!" she determinedly responded, "A company is seeking Community Sales Representatives who have a Community Nursing background - you would be great at that - you could sell ice to an Eskimo! Why don't you apply?" "Ok", I reluctantly said and set about requesting an application form and returning it with a great deal of trepidation. Suppose I am called in for interview? I thought, Ah well, if it is meant to be it will all work out right for me! After all – I had been quite successful as a local "Avon lady".

Sure enough within a few days of sending in my application, I was called to an interview at a hotel. Suitably smart attire was put together and off I went, feeling extremely nervous. Sylvia was totally out of her comfort zone again. On arrival, I was greeted by two friendly and warm natured gentlemen who ushered me into a small meeting room in the hotel, set out with a coffee table and three comfortable armchairs. "Take a seat and relax" I was told as they relaxed back into their chairs. Oh my goodness! This was not what I had expected. Nursing interviews were almost military precision with a panel behind a desk behaving quite brusquely and formally – the chair strategically placed the other side of the desk, so they could fire questions at you and be totally in control of things. Interview by fear tactics, that was.

So here I am in a totally relaxed environment and not knowing what to do next! The guys soon made me feel comfortable and we chatted for some time and I answered their questions to the best of my ability. At the end of the interview they advised me that I would hear from them within the next few days regarding a second interview.

I waited with bated breath over the next couple of days thinking to myself frequently – "what am I doing? Suppose I am accepted for the job?" A letter arrived within 5 days and I nervously opened it. I froze as I read "We would like you to attend a second interview at out Head Office in Crawley where you will meet the Director and Marketing Director" – Oh Crumbs!! Part of me was ecstatic but part of me was almost sick with fright! I might actually be in a sales position within the next six weeks! What do I wear to such a special interview. My wardrobe did not come up trumps and my budget was tight. A very good friend of mine offered to loan me the money to go and buy a suitable summer outfit as it was a very warm summer. I had never spent mega bucks on an outfit before. Feeling guilty (childhood programming rising) I ventured out to a department store and ended up buying a beautiful Planet summer weight outfit and showed it off to friends with pride. Practicality of course made me determined to get a lot of wear out of it.

The day dawned and off I went to Crawley, and found my way to the head office of a Medical Sundries Company called Sherwood Medical. My mouth was dry with nerves but I felt good in my expensive Planet outfit. Reception were ready for my arrival and I was shown up to the Director's office where I met him and the Marketing Director plus the Area Sales Manager who had been at my first interview. Yes it was quite laid back but more intensive. As I was leaving, the Director posed a question to me which I cannot recall but I do recall giving quite a cheeky response as I walked out of the door. "That's it!" – "I have blown it!" I thought as my nursing programming kicked in. Well, surprise, surprise within 2 days I received a call telling me I had been accepted as a Community Sales Rep. I have to admit I was excited at the prospect now – I would have a company car and expenses allowance. My area manager called me regarding the start date and to give me the choice of car colours – red, white, blue or chocolate brown. Having worked with bowel cancer patients I quickly said to him with a chuckle "Any colour but brown! I have seen enough of that colour over the last five years!" We both laughed down the phone and I decided on red. The day dawned for my commencement and again I went to Head Office and met my colleagues – also ex nurses wanting a career move. We gelled immediately and soon got stuck into the day one training and document filing. We stayed overnight in a local hotel and met company staff for dinner so we could get to know each other better. At the end of the two days it was time to collect one's car and proudly drive it home. There was a new shiny red Ford Sierra waiting for me. The boot was stocked up with goodies and home I drove, falling very quickly in love with my brand new motor.

Thus began 5 happy years of selling into the Health Care Industry. What a difference to my nursing career with its necessary rigid rules and discipline. I remember chatting with my Area Sales Manager and asking him about things like arranging hair appointments that I had previously done during my off duty days or on my way home. His reply was so out of character to what I was used too. "Well" he stated "I don't know about you – but my hair grows during working time, doesn't yours?" In other words, be sensible and fit it in around business calls. The sense of freedom to be myself was now emerging and I loved driving throughout the Essex area of town and country going to meet Community Nurses, Nursing Homes and Pharmacists. I was well received because of my Nursing background. As confidence in my integrity grew with the Nurses I met, a sales call would begin with coffee and Sylvia being a listener and counsellor for at least 25 minutes and then the promotion was easy as I was being a friend rather than just another "Rep". I really knew I had impacted and gained trust when I could "drop in" and be well received. "Put the kettle on for coffee Sylvia" was the greeting and then ensued the usual listening and empathy session. For me it was all about "selling but not selling". It is known that customers usually "buy" the Representative first and then the product, because mutual trust is established.

Pharmacy visits were initially greeted very frostily but Sylvia's charm won them over and before long I was sitting in the back, drinking tea and chatting whilst they filled prescription orders. On gaining my confidence, they would then agree to stock the product for the Nurses and Nursing Homes.

A overnight stay in the hotel was sometimes necessary so that a productive day's work could be achieved – drive to the territory early the first day and do some visits, stay over and consolidate business and then drive home for a late finish to the day. Nurses would come and say "You're lucky! Good salary, company car and you get to stay in hotels!" Believe me, the novelty soon wore off and evenings on one's own in a hotel with meals and a book became a little boring.

Selling into the Health Industry was fun but also very challenging. Most of the products they used were on a yearly contract basis offering companies the opportunity to bid. In the sundries products area, this was then very often done on price alone regardless of the overall quality of the product. To get your product into the system meant meeting Specialist Nurses, Team Leaders or arranging Community Nurse lunches and leaving samples for them to "try out". This was followed up and then the challenge began to get them to place a "non-stock" order – they are going against the yearly contract or stocked items – alert either the hospital supplies officer or the Community Pharmacy and get them on your side to order the products in. With a lot of leg work and P.R. the Community could be a lucrative market. The Nursing background certainly helped as the trust was there that you would only sell a product you believed in.

I recall entering a territory in North London where a major competitor had been holding their own for years and used what constituted to bribery with supplies officers and Consultants to get products accepted on a contract. My determination came to the fore and I almost lived on the territory day and night to get product in – Specialist Nurse rapport building followed by trials in a chosen hospital which meant trials for day staff and night staff with tasty cakes and drinks provided to get them in the mood for a friendly promotion. There is nothing quite like doing a product presentation with enthusiasm (to keep awake) around 2.00 a.m. in the morning with Nurses also feeling the body clock trying to take over. Thank goodness for some intertwined humorous stories. It took two and a half years to get product accepted and some sales to begin chipping away at the competition and be on the annual contract. There were always a few nurses who declared "The products are not very good – they don't work!" Delving more deeply, it was clear that the training Sylvia had given had not been passed on as requested and the product was therefore perfectly efficient if used correctly. One such product was a urinary sheath for men – a bit like a condom with a hole at the end and short tube to connect to a drainage bag. Success was due to directing and following guidelines. Try and put the sheath on without following the instructions on the leaflet would surely bring disaster! A bit like home appliances where one is so keen to get on with things the instructions are ignored. Very soon we cry "This is not much good! – the such and such does not work!!!" Try reading the instructions!!!

Life is also a bit like this too. We come with our inner guide or consciousness that is ready to help us on our journey through life but with programming we think we know better by using the EGO (Edging God Out) part of our mind which can easily take us in the wrong direction. We then complain that things are not going right, when, if we had gone within and brought the inner knowing, though the ego mind to outer experience challenges would be better surmounted or accepted as a learning experience for the higher self as it experiences through the dense physical form. As I write this, I am aware that this is the time of awakening the eternal self within mankind which can facilitate a universal healing due to earthly life experience being expressed with love and a greater community co-operation.

Chapter 2

In At The Deep End!

After two and a half years selling sundry items related to the specialist nursing and renal care health sector, I applied for a sales position with a company new to the UK and part of an Australian Medical Glove Company. The goal was to chip away at a leading surgical glove market with a unique concept of medical glove that gave strength and sensitivity in the key areas to assist surgeons with dexterity during operation procedures. This was indeed another challenge – organising trials in theatre settings and covering a territory from Kent to Dorset. I worked with a great team of Sales Representatives and soon settled into the task at hand.

It was Christmas time in my first six months and I was assigned a task by the UK Sales and Marketing Director which related to past experience. "Please will you research the Community Glove Market side and bring a report to the early January Sales Meeting?" "Sure" I replied, gasping within myself. How on earth was Sylvia going to gather in information between Christmas and New Year? Well - there were no excuses, as this information was to be passed on to the European Sales and Marketing Director so that we could plan a strategy for the community market. I spent Christmas with friends as I was not in a relationship at this time and then set to work. However, this was indeed a challenging task as I had enjoyed a really indulgent Christmas, still somewhat unaware of my food intolerance. Two days after Boxing Day when I planned to start phone calls, I woke with a Migraine to end all Migraines! Prostrate on the sofa, with a notebook and pen in hand, I began making phone calls with a head that seemed to have completely "fried my brain". This continued as I worked over the next few days up to New Year. How I wanted to curl up in bed and let the Migraine take its course in the darkness! In spite of my symptoms, somehow I managed to gather the information ready to speedily put into a format, acceptable to the bosses.

January dawned and the meeting day was looming. In the nick of time I was ready to present my report. This was accepted with great praise and the Sales Representative from Scotland was very impressed as he had migrated across from our leading competitor. At the end of the meeting I was called to the UK Sales and Marketing Director's Office – old nursing habit of fear kicks in – "Have I done something wrong?" I thought – What a shock I got when I was highly praised and asked if I would take the position of UK Product Manager as the current one was leaving! So here I am, ready to jump in at the deep end and take on responsibility for the UK Marketing and P.R. campaigns, plus liaise with Europe and our manufacturers in Malaysia and Sri Lanka.

Day one of the new position dawns and I am shown into my office which has a computer on the desk, "I am not computer literate", I whisper to my Secretary, "Don't worry" she kindly replied – it is all menu driven and the information you will need is all programmed in. I do all your typing and letters etc. plus there is a tuition programme as well to help. I breathe a sigh of relief and then go into the UK Sales and Directors' Office for my first meeting and to have my duties as Product Manager explained. Thus began nearly 3 years of never stop fun, exhaustion and major "out of comfort zone" experiences. Our Scottish Sales Representative who had been in Marketing with the competitor offered to help me as much as he could. "You only have to ask" he told me.

A great life and success lesson here. Don't try and do it all yourself. Find an expert and have the courage to ask for help. It shows strength and tenacity and not weakness. All successful people find others to help their vision become reality. One person cannot know everything and do everything. Teamwork is the key. As I settled into my new role the days became extremely busy with hours expanding as deadlines for reports to Europe have to be met plus liaison with our manufacturer in Malaysia. The language barrier offers challenges as the first person to answer the phone might often be one of the workers whose English was as good as non-existent. The solution was to just say the Production Managers name only and they understood you needed to speak with him.

It took a while for me to get used to working with a secretary after doing all my own paperwork and booking my own appointments. "That's my job not yours!" a voice would cry, with a hint of laughter from outside my office.

The European head office was in the city of Munich and there were regular day trips for important meetings plus attendance of exhibitions to assist with promotion in German Cities. I saw little of the cities as it was usually – arrive at the airport, hail a cab and go straight to the hotel which was only a short distance from the exhibition hall. Evenings were spent dining with friendly Germans and trying to understand their conversations. I did teach myself some basic German with a BBC video and cassette tutor so that I could at least greet people. Plus say goodnight as well. In eating places I could just about request food in German and impress those around! They made a good friend of me when I visited as I was trying to blend in as much as I could whilst there. English of course had to be spoken in Head office, as demanded by the European Sales and Marketing Director.

Refraining from too much alcohol, was one of my challenges as most of the team did like to drink with great relish and seemed to enjoy discussing who had the worst hangover the next morning. Not quite my idea of fun! I would rather have few and wake up without a sore head and nausea – two very heavy drinking sessions in my twenties was enough for me! Sylvia can have as much fun as the rest without the aid of alcohol and the side effects. I recall being at a wedding and someone actually making a comment "Look at Sylvia having a really great time and without a drop of alcohol" One glass of wine seems quite sufficient for my physical body now and that, only occasionally. Oh! I am not preaching sobriety here by the way – although I do now believe that if we are at peace with who we truly are – a spiritual being living out experiences through a dense physical body temple – then that inner joy freely expresses itself without the aid of a drug (alcohol is considered to be another form of a drug). As I write this, I can recall a few of my patients in my busy days who firmly believed that their healthy longevity was linked to their tot of whiskey or brandy before retiring.

In At The Deep End!

The key memory with this company, related to planning and organisation of our launch of a brand new surgical glove for those allergic to latex, at the Theatre Nurses exhibition in Harrogate. My oh my! That was a week – stamina plus plus was required to stay the pace from Sunday to Friday morning – thankfully the final stages of setting up the stand on Sunday went well and everyone involved, relaxed over a meal in the hotel and wine etc. etc.!!! Determined to be 100% alert for an 8.00 a.m. start on the stand I went to bed a lot earlier than most of the team who arrived at our stand looking "careworn" on Monday morning. "Will they stay the course?" I asked myself – somehow they did with high doses of caffeine during the day and alcohol in the evenings, the sessions going on until the early hours of the morning. It was considered good practice to mix with the nurses attending the exhibition, many of whom were staying at the same hotel – free from home ties and work pressures. The nurses were ready for a good time and company expense bills grew by the day!

On Wednesday evening we had put together our "Special Evening" complete with free bar and food along with limbo dancing for entertainment. Fairly soon into the evening the UK Sales and Marketing Director along with the European Sales and Marketing Director were far from sober and at 9.00 p.m. one of the waiters came over to me and stated "Sylvia you do realise all the nurses are ordering cocktails!!!!" This was the time to officially stop the free drinks. However, the two Sales and Marketing Directors decreed in their "very happy" state "Oh keep the bar going for another hour!" Sylvia made absolutely sure that cocktails were not on the drinks menu from then on. I was cringing at the thought of where the marketing budget for the week was going to end up! The evening was a success in spite of the "hidden" dilemmas and I recall eventually getting to bed around 2.00 a.m. wondering how I was going to stay the pace till the end of the week. Caffeine and alcohol were "in moderation" with my food intolerance. Well, surprise, surprise I was up and at the stand on time and the rest of the team crawled in around 9.00 a.m. looking absolutely wrecked, pale faced and almost proud of their hangovers! Thankfully this was the last day to be "on top form" as tomorrow, Friday all the nurses departed and we only had to undress the stand and take essentials back in our case.

Part of our exhibition stand display was helium filled balloons as well as give away balloons to the nurses which were again filled with helium. As we were undressing the stand a couple of our male field representatives were ready for some last minute fun triggered by overtiredness and a desire to give us all a laugh to relieve the pressure of the week. Untying some of the balloons, they inhaled the helium and had us in hysterics of laughter as they spoke in high pitched voices that sounded like "Daffy Duck" from the television programme.

It was a very long drive home and every service station was visited for a "pick me up" drink and short "power nap" to prevent me falling asleep whilst driving. How I was looking forward to getting back to my cosy flat in Surrey! Little did I know a challenge was to await me – another experience that would increase my empathy with future clients.

Parking the car with great relief, I struggled up the stairs to my front door ready to just dump everything, have a quick drink and fall into bed. I looked at the front door through exhausted eyes and thought that something was not quite right with the door. How right I was, the front door had been forced open and on entering my flat saw it had been ransacked and burgled. The only person I could think to call, as I was new to the area, was my good friend and boss from work. Bless her, she immediately came over and the police soon arrived. Dusting for fingerprints everywhere, taking my fingerprints for elimination and general observation to find the entry route was carried out. They left after finding out that one of the downstairs flats had been entered via the kitchen window and exited via the front door to get to my flat after looking around their dwelling. We decided to drown our sorrows and I ended up drinking almost a bottle of quality red wine and collapsing into bed late that evening. An appointment had been arranged for early morning to fit a temporary front door so there was not time for Sylvia to stay in bed till late and recover from the night before. Somehow I managed to stay upright and talk to the carpenter, whilst enduring an intense headache plus nausea as the thought constantly arose "Hurry up and do the job and get going!" He was such a pleasant and friendly chap who enjoyed conversing plus drinking regular cups of coffee whilst he worked. No problem for Sylvia on any other occasion but today – where is the guy who just wants to arrive, do the job and leave as quickly as possible?

Although little was seemingly taken, I was "on edge" for a few months to come, and kept finding that "something else" was missing. Thankfully, not of great monetary value, but some sentimental value. Isn't it interesting how we attach ourselves to the material things around us when ultimately we will leave this physical life and return to the beautiful place from whence our soul comes to experience. Over time, Sylvia has become less attached to material things and regularly de-clutters. Feng Shui teaches the power of physical de-cluttering to aid in the de-cluttering of old patterns and emotions that have no place in our progression on the earthly journey. I have great admiration for Dr Wayne Dyer who prior to taking a year out to live in the Tao, totally cleared his office of everything, including awards he had been given.

Chapter 3

The Camping Years

Life was never "all work and no play" and regular summer holidays and fun activities were a part of life's rich pattern. My budget being tight, it was decided that myself and friends would indulge in camping holidays. Sylvia began subscribing to the Camping Magazine to get tips about how to get the best out of your camping experience – it had to be done properly like anything else in life.

So where do we buy a tent? We need a 2 – 3 bedroomed frame tent. There were also children going to accompany us, as my best friend had a daughter and we always took a couple of friends of hers with her. They were keen to have their own tent so that was budgeted for as well. After much researching, we bought a second hand tent that needed waterproofing but was a good size with front and back entrances, space for a camping stove and at least two bedroom areas. Living in a flat at the time, a garden was needed to erect the tent and paint it with waterproofing paint. Another kind friend offered their garden and off we went with great excitement, having been assured that the tent poles were colour coded and instructions were provided – we set about the task of putting up the tent frame. Sylvia was confident having read her camping magazines, that all would go smoothly. As the tent poles were excitedly taken out of the net bag there is a general sigh of disbelief. None of the tent poles were colour coded and we had no instructions!!!! Time passed and we were still struggling, when a gentleman a few doors down saw us from his garden and offered to help. The "quickly up with the tent and get it painted" had been an arduous day long venture. A good sense of humour and determination saw the tent successfully erected and painting began. The colour had faded, so blue waterproof paint had been purchased and paint brushes gathered between us. Amid many cups of tea and refreshments, plus of course dry weather, which is always a gamble here in the U.K., the tent was painted and drying quickly in the sun. Paint was also drying nicely on the painters as well. Never mind! A good shower would deal with that later. A final refreshment break took place inside the tent to celebrate it's launch into action. By the next day, the paint had dried and it was time to dismantle the tent and label all the poles so that we would easily erect the tent on its first voyage into action. By the time we had decided on our "basic equipment", a trailer was needed to carry all the equipment which included a rug to go inside the tent, heater for cold and wet weather, and portable T.V. Being born in the month of July and a reasonably typical Cancerian, Sylvia knew how to create "home from home".

The first of many trips were organised down into the West Country and of course the dog came too, a cheeky West Highland Terrier bitch called Whiskey. The plan had been to have two dogs called Whiskey and Soda but only one puppy was left when we went to purchase – so Whiskey was the name kept and the Soda forgotten, no doubt. Fairly confident, regarding my knowledge of first time camping from diligent magazine reading, Sylvia became a natural "camping leader". "Right", I excitedly instructed as we drove into the camp site – "we must first of all find as level a pitch as possible, to erect the tent". What was considered the best area was chosen and the tent proudly lifted out of the trailer. Grand inspection began to ensure we had chosen the very best place. After about 20 minutes it must have been obvious to other "regular campers" that we were novices and a male voice roared across the field "Are you going to put the b****y tent up or not?" Embarrassed, we set to work and the gentleman came across and helped us, stating that reading magazines was not the answer but to get out there and erect the tent. If it suddenly rains there is no time to run around inspecting the land!!!

Thus began at least 7 years of fun camping in the South West of England and the Isle of Wight.

1976 was a great year for camping as the weather was positively "Riveria" temperatures. There is nothing quite like a full English breakfast under a clear blue sky with the early sun beating down. Some mornings

Whiskey would sneak out early and we would wonder where she was. "It is alright" a voice would call from the next door tent, "she is having her breakfast". The smell of bacon and sausages cooking had been too much for her nose and of course our camping neighbours had taken to her and were happy to indulge her, much to our embarrassment. Being an early riser by nature, on some mornings I would wake up and organise the children; gather some cereal, milk and some cold drinks and pile us all, along with Whisky into the car and go to the beach at about 8.00 a.m. as it was warm enough to be in shorts and a t shirt. Pre-breakfast on the beach was great fun and Whiskey had her own bowl of drink too. This was usually then attempted to be temporarily buried in the sand completely covering the dish and water. She obviously did not wish to indulge in drinking so early – a swim in the sea was more exciting. The kids enjoyed our time together on the beach and we left, just as the crowds began to arrive to be greeted back at the tent with a cooked breakfast before going on a day trip somewhere on the Island. Evenings were spent sitting outside the tent after the children retired in their tent. Wine and cards was the order of the night and our neighbours joined us too. By 10.30 p.m. or sometimes 11.00 p.m. we eventually decided it was time to find our way to the toilets and retire to bed. Some evenings at around 10.15 p.m. we were "entertained" by campers opposite who had dined in style with tablecloth and wine glasses earlier and would undress in the tent by dimmed lighting and we could see silhouettes and movement as the lady undressed. We tried our best to be quiet and not laugh and we did not have the heart to tell her that she was entertaining the campsite each evening.

One year we were privileged to be in a field adjacent to the farmers cattle field – a cow was due to give birth at any time and we hoped we would be able to witness the event. Good early reproduction education for the children! Sure enough one morning the routine of the day was overruled as the cow was very much in labour and crying out with "Moo Moo" as contractions became greater. "Quickly" I called to the children with dog on the lead after a visit to the "doggy loo" field. "A calf will soon arrive" Eventually the calf began to appear and with a little help from the farmer, fell to the ground and was licked by her mother to stimulate breathing and standing on its feet. We watched with bated breath as the calf attempted to stand up struggling for over twenty minutes, and then – hooray! – it stood up and instinctively went to its mothers teats for its first drink. Overjoyed at witnessing the wonderful moment we then continued our day. By the next morning, the calf and its mother were doing very well, but of course, we had to go and have a look each day to watch the progress during the final days of our stay. These were happy times and I was enjoying life with my good friends and exploring new ways of looking at spirituality. A not so joyous occasion, whilst camping one year on the Isle of Wight, was when we were packing up the tent. I stooped down to pull out one of the corner tent pegs and the next thing everyone is witnessing Sylvia hopping round the field on her left leg shouting out words a lot stronger than Ouch!! I had trodden on a tent peg that had been sheared in half by a previous camper!! It had gone into the bottom of my foot and out again!! The pain was indescribable and to make matters worse, I was the main driver, happy to tow a trailer behind a hired Vauxhall Victor Estate to accommodate everyone. The foot began to swell which meant a visit to hospital for a tetanus injection, antibiotics, pain killers and a dressing with a follow up on arrival at home. One of my friends had recently passed her driving test and drew the short straw for driving us home. We arrived home safe and sound and my foot healed within a couple of weeks with rest and no driving.

This period of my life brought me into contact with the Gay Community and weekly disco's were a "must" on the calendar every Friday night! There was a good deal of "camping" here too, I can tell you, and many friends were made during this time. Special nights were arranged with entertainment and the famous "Lily Savage" was one of the regular entertainers, before making it into the big time. The fancy dress parties that went on and annual discos in the barns of one of the "boys" farms, were outrageous affairs and went on till at least 2.00 a.m. in the morning. Thankfully, there were no immediate neighbours to disturb. Amongst the friends made, was a guy who was a very Spiritual and powerful Medium and it was he who channelled a message from Mother after she passed into the Spirit world. Interacting with gay men and women plus transgenders and cross dressers, enabled me to more fully understand the wider spectrum of humanity and accept people for the spiritual beings they were, living through this physical form with all it's challenges and judgements of human kind. I know I may be challenging some readers here, but a better lesson in understanding and acceptance, Sylvia could not have had as she observed genuinely lovely and caring people struggling to live out who they were, in a world so judgemental around sexuality. If we are interconnected with each other as spiritual beings as part of the universal source essence then surely we need to embrace this part of all human kind. How else will we bring true peace to Mother Earth if we do not release judgement of others? There are enough challenges to live out who we truly are, without taking on others agendas. Let others choose who they wish to be and experience their life and pour pure love to all human kind – plus animals and all of Mother Earth of course – and allow choices to be made. A catalyst for my final acceptance of the way God and the Master Jesus could guide my Spiritual path and Life Purpose.

Chapter 4

Disillusionment – What is Next?

Time passed and I was becoming restless within myself and wanting change. My health was reasonable and I had been re-awakened in my inner self through a dear friend and Mentor whilst living in Kent. It had seemed that whatever I did and wherever Sylvia went in her life, there was something missing – a purpose unfulfilled that ordinary earthly pleasures could not satisfy. I had always felt different somehow.

Sitting in a meditation circle whilst being in Kent had stimulated a desire to re-connect with my soul/spirit self and rekindle an inner joy that I had experienced when I had my encounter with the Master Jesus at the age of ten. The way this happened was uncanny and of course not by "chance".

Prior to my stepping out into the business world Daddy passed into God's World of Spirit and I was devastated. I felt as if a part of me was gone and grieved him for a long time, but tried to hide my grief so as to help Mummy. She was a very "deep" soul and never expressed emotions publicly so I never knew how she was really feeling. It was during this period of my life that I was being drawn to the more "spiritual" way of life where it was considered perfectly normal to have loved ones communicate from the Spirit World where they now lived on, free of the dense physical form. My mother being still very linked into her Pentecostal Religion, could not accept this. One day I was visiting her and she told me that Daddy had appeared to her at the living room doorway. "Oh!" I said "I expect he came to see that you were alright and to show you he was fine now". Nothing more was said and I left wondering how she dealt with the experience when the religion taught, was that we must not communicate with people after they had died. Daddy, I feel wanted her to learn something of a reality of life in the Spirit World. Sylvia's experience with Daddy still stays with her to this day -

It was about six months after Daddy passed into Spirit and I had a really vivid "dream" experience. I was in a beautiful garden of a large mansion house and Daddy was with me looking just like he did when he was healthy on earth. We went into the afternoon tea room and had tea and toasted tea cakes together – they were really scrumptious too. Afterwards we walked into the garden together and I felt so happy and free. "Daddy can I stay here with you?" I asked "No" he responded sharply "Get back down to earth! You have a lot of work to do!" Then like a bullet from a gun I leapt through the back of my bed and found myself in my physical body again. I did not fully understand what he meant yet, but I knew it was linked to a life purpose I was to fulfil.

Around six to twelve months later I had another experience with Daddy. We were sitting together in the kitchen of my childhood home. He was showing in full "physical" form and I could almost touch him. There was radiance around him and his teeth shone with brightness – all of a sudden I felt a feeling of love within and around me that was and is, indescribable. "What is this feeling?" I asked Daddy "This is all the love in the Spirit World" he replied and a few seconds later I was catapulted back into my physical body. The feeling stayed with me for many days just as I had felt it, when with Daddy. It was as if I experienced the love of all creation in its perfection and I knew that no love on earth could ever match this unless it was true unconditional spiritual essence manifesting in a relationship. As I have since talked about and reflected on this amazing experience, it is very clear to me that the greatest love is indeed within us, as we are all part of that great universal love that we separate ourselves from through programming during our time here on earth. From that moment on, I vowed to seek how to truly find and live out my purpose in life – to help others find who they truly are and live that out through daily life here on earth. As predicted by my friend and Spiritual Mentor I ended up back in the nursing environment. However, just prior to that and two years almost to the day, was when Mummy passed into Gods Spirit

Disillusionment – What is Next?

World suddenly. This left me with a great deal of "unfinished business" and sought counselling from a spiritual counsellor for around 3 years before I fully began to come to terms with her passing. I knew she would be with Daddy and wondered how she was adjusting to her new life after her beliefs she had lived out for many years. Guilt about my new way of spirituality rose up in me from time to time causing inner conflict but my encounters with Daddy re-assured me.

Then one fateful evening, Sylvia went along to an evening of clairvoyance that a well respected spiritual medium and good friend was participating in. Was I taken aback, when half way through the evening, he pointed to me and said "I do not normally go to friends as I know a lot about them, but my guide Charlie would not let it go". He then proceeded to tell me things that my Mummy would only have known and described her to me and traits she had. Oh! Wow! This released my guilt about the path I was on. It was obvious that Mummy had come and communicated so that I would accept the calling to serve through the "spiritual" pathway rather than strict religion. Dedicated healing soon began with my dear little Mentor – yes she was barely five foot tall! Of course I was somewhat discreet about my beliefs as the majority would not understand or were programmed not to believe in "communication with the dead".

Happy now I was beginning my Life Purpose journey, day to day living continued around my spiritual awakening. Yes – Nursing returned and I was accepted to run a Nursing Home in Surrey which was a delightful yet extremely stressful three years for Sylvia. Trying to keep a high standard of care at all times, maintain the nursing staffing levels, ensure relatives were nurtured plus run a profitable business, caused many a sleepless night. This time was another great learning experience and taught Sylvia a lot about teamwork and handling different personalities. It is important to remember:-

* Never enter the kitchen, unless invited by the chef. They have very volatile moods. One of the group Chefs – not in my home, was sacked, due to getting angry at a staff member whilst threateningly holding a meat clever.
* Always check the menstrual cycle or when HRT patches are due with the female members of staff. It helps to understand their

irrational behaviour on certain days. If a female staff member had a very "Off" day the question was asked "when is your patch due?" Sure enough, in the next two or three days. The challenge was that it was "patch renewal time" for one member each week!

* Keep laundry rules strictly observed and clothing "easy-care", machine washable.

One resident's daughter insisted her mother wore the very best in Jaeger, totally unsuitable for the usual laundry process and needed very delicate hand washing or cleaning. Following two unfortunate incidents, where a beautiful red Jaeger sweater was machine washed and tumble dried by a night carer – they were only supposed to do essential lines overnight – and shrank it to the size of a three year olds jumper. How did one explain this away to an understandably enraged daughter? We tried of course to replace the garment. A sigh of relief all around the day the daughter arrived with a large linen basket complete with a notice to go on the wall above it. "PLEASE PUT ALL MOTHERS CLOTHES IN THE LINEN BASKET" "I will do Mothers washing from now on!" (the curt remark was made as she proudly placed the basket in her mother's bedroom).

These incidents were rare and we had a great atmosphere in the home and generally speaking, relatives were happy with the service given.

Part of the day to day life in the Nursing Home was activities for the residents. We had a lovely lady who spread happiness throughout the place when she was on duty. Being an artist herself, she taught me how to see beauty in a cloud and also in rain puddles. Her challenge was in getting residents to participate and not just "sit" with the television on whilst they went into a sleepy haze. I admired her creativity and tenacity to keep producing new things for the residents to do.

A company minibus was available to take residents on trips out to the theatre or picnics in the fine weather. On such outings, Matron volunteered to help. A week prior, a list was drawn up of those who wanted to have an afternoon drive out to a local beauty spot for tea and cakes. The day dawned and final arrangements were in place. Chef had prepared sandwiches and cakes and all was packed up ready to go. The Maintenance man had filled the minibus with petrol and was ready to drive us on our "adventure" - 2 p.m. and it is time to set off. Carers began rounding up residents who to our surprise said "I am not going out! I'll catch cold!" It took much cajoling and patience to get them all into the minibus but once on our way and singing, they all cheered up. We arrived at our destination in good spirits and unloaded. One lady kept us all and the general public entertained by striding out, taking deep breaths and loudly insisting "Let's all take nice deep breaths and breathe in Gods good air!" This was repeated with each great stride and had people around us staring and laughing. Refreshments were served and all seemed to be having a good time. The tea soon went to the bladder and we took over the public toilets to change pads and assist with bladder relieving! Homewood bound then and back to daily routine at the care home. There were many "tales" derived from my time here. It illustrates beautifully, how we can choose to deal with life's day to day issues that occur.

Sylvia is now very much on a spiritual and personal development growth and living day to day with an attitude of gratitude and most times seeing the positive aspect of things. One very kind and efficient Nursing Sister, would greet me regularly, when I arrived in the morning, after they have been on night duties, with the standard greeting of - "Matron we have lots of problems here this morning" to which I would firmly respond - "In my nursing home we do not have problems, only challenges which we will overcome – now come on, we will look at how we will deal with the challenges that need resolving" A sigh and shrug of the shoulders followed, as she followed me to the office for "tea and talk". Bless her, she was programmed to always look for problems in life and not solutions to challenges, yet she was a great asset to the Home and a very religious lady too. So in spite of our differences, I valued her input and had great respect for her.

People will cross our path in life who are different and have different values and we sometimes have to stand our ground, according to our own positive values but that does not mean we allow competitiveness to creep in. When we value others and understand where they are coming from, but state that we just see things differently and that is OK, it can dissipate and prevent an argument. All because we valued them whilst standing in our own power.

It was whilst working at the Care Home that Sylvia finally found the answer to her health issues and had no need for painkillers and anti-nausea drugs to relieve migraine headaches every 3 weeks or so –

One day a lovely woman called in who was a qualified Reflexologist requesting to offer treatments for the residents. Now much more into Holistic therapies, following many years having Homeopathic remedies to improve health and wellbeing, Sylvia accepted her offer. Matron was offered a free treatment – of course this was accepted readily. Regular treatments then became part of Sylvia's life routine. During a review session I was asked about my Migraines and Bowel symptoms in more detail. Immediately the question arose as to whether Sylvia had ever considered seeing a Qualified Nutritional Expert. "No" was the quick answer. "Well, I think your symptoms are more than likely food related" she replied "Would you be interested in my referring you to one of the top UK Nutritionalists. She has treated fringe royalty and other famous people. I'll leave her phone number for you." "Thank you", I replied with an inner sigh of relief that I may have at long last found the answer to my years of suffering!! I eagerly made an appointment and drove all the way to Tooting in South London where I met a slim, dark haired lady with a lovely gentle manner. Her consulting room had signed pictures of famous people such as "Mr Motivator" who used to do exercise routines on UK Breakfast Television. A long six page questionnaire was completed and I returned the following week to be told I had classic wheat and dairy intolerance. I was handed a long list of foods I could eat and those to eliminate. "OK" I thought "If this will solve my problems I'll run with it". With commitment and determination, I set about a revolutionary dietary change creating menu charts and experimenting with recipes. No easy way then, as supermarkets didn't stock the appropriate products. As always, if Sylvia is determined then we do it properly or not at all. No gradual introduction – just do it! This meant a few months of "cold turkey" as I walked past Bakers Shops with the smell of fresh bread wafting towards my nostrils and iced buns and jam donuts tempting me in the window display! Never mind the Ice Cream Van down at the coast with its ice cream cornets staring at me. Ice Lollies just don't do it for the taste buds! It was worth it, as in six weeks I was a new woman minus migraines plus more energy. What was also interesting, was the permanent feeling of butterflies in my solar plexus after eating completely disappeared – felt really strange for a while!

Sylvia still maintains a strict dietary regime generally, but does occasionally "sin" with non gluten free products and overload sugar intake. Still, "moderation in all things" it is said.

I feel I must ask a question at this point – Why do humans expect to improve health without taking responsibility for it? If something is desired in life we sometimes have to be prepared to pay a price for it, whilst seeing the benefit from doing that.

Back at the Nursing Home Sylvia would challenge Chef for meal creativity and was now into herbal teas instead of high caffeine drinks. I recall one morning when a fairly new Carer was keen to impress Matron and knocked on the office door, where I was head down into essential paperwork. "It's coffee round time Matron would you like a drink?" "Yes please – a cup of Chammomile tea would be lovely". Off she trotted and returned with a tray adorned with a cup of greenish white liquid – yes you've guessed – she had put milk in the herbal tea! How do I tell her you don't put milk in herbal teas without upsetting her? "Thank you ….., but I should have told you that herbal teas don't need milk. "Really sorry Matron" She apologised, blushing. "it's OK. You weren't to know" Sylvia caringly responded, and a few minutes later she returned with a perfect cup of herbal tea. She must have told everyone as, never again did a cup of herbal tea appear containing cows milk!

Many more tales could be told but perhaps that is another book!!

Chapter 5

Organised Chaos!

In life, situations occur that seem unfair and chaotic at the time, yet they are the catalyst for take-off with one's Life Purpose. This was the case with Sylvia. I believe that life IS ALWAYS IN DIVINE ORDER no matter what is going on around us, in our experience of the moment. Let me explain – one fatal day – yet not really fatal, Sylvia had been to the dentist and prior to that drawn out a small amount of cash from the Care Home Residents fund. Feeling unwell from the local anaesthetic – Sylvia was sensitive to a number of things with her food intolerance - a decision was made to call the Care Home and ensure all was well and return to my home and relax. The next morning I went to work as usual but had omitted to take the residents monies and the building society book with me. Knowing it would be safe where I had left it in the house, plus the monies not required that day, a decision was made to ensure it was brought in the next day and routine went on as usual. I left the Care Home around 4.45 p.m. and returned home to find that we had been burgled and as well as some precious items, the resident's monies and building society book had also been stolen. Immediately, I alerted our Head Office to the effect and confirmed that the Police were to be informed. Fortunately it was only around fifty pounds that was missing. If necessary, I was prepared to personally replenish the monies for the residents. Life continued and my partner and I went away for a week as planned. On my return, I found a letter had been delivered and I was requested to go to Head Office for a meeting. It suddenly became clear to me, that certain actions I had taken, dealing with the delicate staffing issues early on, at the Care Home as

Manager, were not really appreciated and I was not as popular as appeared. A full disciplinary hearing ensued with the cash disappearance being one of the list of petty items that were stacked against Sylvia. Although my confidence had grown over the years the deeply programmed fear of authority rose up as questions were thrown at me. I allowed myself to create fear and confusion around the issues ensued. The outcome was immediate suspension from duty and in 3 months I was paid to leave. The experience was a painful one as I witnessed my partner being both angry at how I was treated plus "You must have done something wrong!" By the time I was leaving, a new Director of Nursing was in place who ensured that a good reference was given and wondered what all the nonsense was about and said it should never have happened. This was a great learning curve for Sylvia and from then on, the old pattern of fear of authority really did begin to dissipate.

I have since then, seen the blessing of the whole saga and it taught me great empathy to those experiencing redundancy or disciplinary hearings without judgement. Although a drastic time, there was Divine organisation behind the whole scenario. Sylvia went on to find further employment with a Specialist Community Nursing/Sales company and at interview took full control as my boss later laughingly stated "Actually You Interviewed The Boss!!!" A bit of a turnaround eh?

Some would wonder why I chose to work in the area of "incontinence", but it opened my eyes to the problem in society with both men and women and the stigma attached. I studied a course and received the appropriate accreditation. The course involved working alongside Specialist Nurses for this problem and I soon realised that society at large has no idea what many suffer as a result of being incontinent. The only piece of equipment for helping alleviate things, was in gadgets advertised in the typical small catalogues that sell via the post that appear on the doormat. Who wants to admit they have such a problem? My role was to visit males who had an incontinence issue, recommend and fit an appropriate "gadget" which could be allowed on prescription. I recall one gentleman I went to assess around 11am in the morning. He, like many had been housebound for a number of years and after successfully "sorting him out" and arranging a follow up visit, as I was leaving he grabbed his coat and walking stick." Where are you off too?" I smilingly requested. "I'm going down the pub!

Not had a drink there for a few years!!" On my follow up visit, I met a "happy chappy" who was out daily and coping well with his new "device" He was one of many I encountered during my time with the company. What WAS interesting was explaining to friends and family at functions what I was doing for a living!! I did my best to be discreet and usually the conversation ended up with seeing humour in the tragedy. One of my colleagues working in the East Anglia area, had an embarrassing moment when sadly her car was involved in an accident and the Police were called. A replacement car was to be delivered so she could continue working. This meant emptying the boot of the car which was full of gadgets for incontinence of all shapes and sizes. As the Police helped her unload there were a few very "choice" comments made about what she might be doing with the male clients which lightened the disaster and caused great hilarity!

From now on Sylvia was to have a variety of Private Nursing employments, including Agency Community Nursing for a number of years as she became hungry for and progressed on her Spiritual Life Purpose Path.

Through a work colleague I was introduced to the Network Marketing Industry and thus began an arrival at the "Personal Development and Success Training School." Also the entrepreneurial Spirit was rising and a determination to succeed in life without the standard "Nine to Five" job. Some small success has been achieved in this industry but somehow something deep within was holding Sylvia back. It was as if there was deep rooted programming and Karmic issues to be weeded out. "How do those that make mega bucks in this industry do it?" was frequently mentally asked, whilst prospecting everyone with three feet of myself and failing to get the numbers in my "downline". However, I was enjoying being around people who believed in success and purpose in life and many had their own spiritual philosophy they lived by, as well. It was through this industry I met the key people who would help me forge ahead on my Life Purpose Path which was beyond Nursing and the orthodox Medical Establishment.

Chapter 6

It's Time To "Take Off"

My work as a channelling Medium was growing and a desire to use healing powers I was blessed with years ago in my youth, wanted to be expressed.

Of course it was essential to qualify in a recognised Spiritual Healing arena. I considered different healing modalities but none seemed to resonate until……

Sitting on my desk near my computer was a business card of a great friend of mine in the Network Marketing Industry – it never seemed to get lost – unlike many I would avidly search for and not find! One day I decided to call him and asked "What are you up to these days" "I am into massage and also a Reiki Master and teach Reiki" Oops!!! Was this a piece of Gods Synchronicity? How was Sylvia going to do healing?

Reiki Healing Therapy, as it was also known, was beginning to get more widely known in the 1990's and something in Sylvia had an "Aha" moment. The decision was made to learn Reiki and the healing power flowed through. "You are a Natural Healer" I was told and during each attunement amazing spiritual connections and visions occurred that both humbled Sylvia and brought tears to the eyes. Life now would never be the same again! Once on the path of Reiki the soul destiny calls and one's own true healing really does take place. Old patterns rise up for release, new doors open for one to walk through which may of course challenge. Yet it is exciting as the Soul rejoices in its opportunity to now fully express its ultimate purpose through the physical body temple.

Marketing myself was the next challenge so that I would gain a client base. Having by now gained some pretty good computer skills through much trial and error, plus determination, I created some simple three fold brochures which I distributed to various outlets. A local Fitness Gym were open to have a Reiki Therapist as the manager was very into the Holistic Arena. I practiced here for well over a year and gained some regular clients who gave good testimony to the power of Reiki. I also did some work at a GP practice at weekends and had a married couple who came every Sunday for their "Reiki Chill". Restaurant owners was their profession, and life was both busy and challenging for them. The husband had high blood pressure which meant regular check-ups with the GP. The "Reiki Hour" had a very positive impact with gradual reduction in the readings which pleased the G.P. After his first session he was so pleased with the relaxing effect he would arrive at the appointment time say "Hello", jump on the couch close his eyes and within seconds the loud snoring echoed through the small building I was working in! At the end of the session he would say "thank you,", pass over the agreed investment, and was on his way. I am sure the energy plus an hour's total sleep relaxation worked in tandem for his blood pressure. His wife would enjoy a short chat and story of his problems before her treatment. She was equally pleased with the positive benefits. Another "home visit" client was the exact opposite with her mode of relaxation. "Can I talk?" she asked as she clambered onto my portable couch "Yes of course" I responded expecting a short extension of the first visit record form. She talked non-stop for the whole hour and I left feeling that I now needed my own Reiki Session to free my brain of that chatter!! However, she did feel the benefit and had some more treatments to re-balance and re-align energies in the physical body as well as assisting with the stress relief. It is a joy and very humbling to witness the power of Healing and see lives change as a result. Healing is not just associated with physical body diseases. The impact on emotional and life issues can be phenomenal. If we acknowledge that it is scientifically known that stress is over 80% of the cause of illness then it makes good sense to deal with emotional issues for health and wellbeing improvement. Emotional healing through the power of Reiki Therapy is best illustrated with another client I was blessed to help whilst working at a different Fitness Centre. She had booked for some Relaxing Reiki and the first appointment "in depth" assessment completed. This would include a scientifically designed Health Profile to assess the balance of the physical body systems, and appropriate Organic Balancing Herbs would be recommended. Usually four treatments were advised to allow some general energy shift and deeper emotional release to take place. Further regular sessions would be discussed and agreed, if the client was keen to progress in improving their health and wellbeing. The client Sylvia recalls, had one specific concern, which we discussed during her assessment and was most definitely totally emotionally associated. She committed to the suggested four treatments and on the fourth session, at the end of the Reiki sat up, burst into tears, said "I get it now!", continuing to express an incident in her teens that had been deeply buried in her subconscious which had influenced recent times in her marriage. She went away on a "high" ready to sort things out at home! Sylvia was moved by this lady's experience and even more in awe of the power of Reiki!

We are all bundles of energy and emotional stress creates blockages in our energy flow which in turn links to the energy balance within the cells of our body. Any imbalance shows itself as physical symptoms which can be alleviated through orthodox medicine routes. Combined with identifying the underlying cause of the symptoms, this inludes empowered relationships………

Chapter 7

Yes – I Found My Soulmate!!

Sylvia's journey from the day she encountered Reiki has been one of tremendous healing and a journey to finally living out her life purpose whereby helping others find within themselves their true self, enabling them to heal and re-create a new empowered life of excitement and fulfilment.

Part of that was to meet the man who Sylvia was to end up marrying – knowing it was part of the Divine plan of my life.

After many years of varying relationships and non-interest in the male species for a time, and after a relationship with a man older than myself and very quickly getting engaged to be married, staying with him for ten years and then realising it wasn't right, a very different gentleman was to walk into my life……..

It was another very ordinary Sunday in my flat and early evening. Sylvia was thinking she might go the local Spiritualist Church Service held every Sunday in a Community Youth Centre. "Shall I go or not?" The service began at 6.30pm and it was now 6.15pm. "Yes! I will!" Luckily it was only a few minutes drive away and arrival was just before the service commenced. Sneaking into the back row I observed the Chairperson following the medium down to the front of the "church". He would be addressing the congregation and channel spiritual messages of comfort and upliftment to members of the congregation through connection to his guides in God's spiritual world, plus loved ones who wished to speak and re-assure they were very much alive in a body free of the denseness of the physical form. This could also be a very healing time as forgiveness took place for things done whilst here on earth and other issues were resolved. The Medium was dressed in a very smart "classic" way and the thought in Sylvia's head was "Ooh! He's nice – probably married with the statutory 2 kids and totally unavailable." He did target me and give me a very accurate spiritual message, which impressed me.

At the end of the service, we were all offered tea and biscuits, plus having a good chat with each other. Whilst drinking my cup of tea and indulging just one very plain biscuit, a voice spoke to me, "Go and talk to the Medium". As no-one was chatting to him, I took myself down to the front and sat down next to him, thanking him for my message earlier and its accuracy. We sat chatting and he realised I too, was a working Medium. Next followed, what I consider the best chat-up line I have ever heard! "You know, we Mediums never seem to get a reading for ourselves." My quite innocent response was "I'll give you a reading sometime if you like" and passed him my business card. Thinking no more of it, I went home and within ten minutes the phone rang – "It's Brian here. I was really enjoying our conversation, can we carry on with it?" My response, I know was not what he had hoped "Sorry, I have a friend coming round tonight. When are you free again for a chat?" Thus followed a brief joint calendar checking between us and both of us were committed to things, for at least two weeks. Even weekends were a no-no as Brian was a Barn Dance Caller with his own band and most Saturdays and some Fridays, they had bookings due to their popularity. I agreed to go for a drink on a weekday evening and looked forward to seeing him. That was also a very interesting evening! Being a Barn Dance caller, I also found out later, he was a dedicated folk fan and sang regularly at folk clubs. No wonder we end up in a pub with a "respectable" Kareoke Night! Well, Brian got up and sung a song and I was amazed and very impressed with the quality of his voice. "Are you going to sing Sylvia?" he asked. Oh My! Some of the old nervousness crept in but my own history of singing - in the school choir, strumming my guitar to gospel songs accompanied by a friend, as well as entertaining friends, overcame all this. I scanned the list of songs and decided to sing Edelweiss from the famous film- The sound of Music. I got a round of applause and suitably impressed my "date". He sang a second song and became the "star" of the evening. "Are you going to sing for us again Sylvia?" I began checking the song list and really did know which to choose. "Come along Sylvia. Hurry up!" curtly rang in my ears. For a split second I thought "What **am** I doing here with this man?" Still, I was keen to impress so decided to sing Hey There Georgie Girl which was made famous by The Seekers. Half way through I had to give up as a fit of coughing set in and I returned to my seat with a sigh of relief! The evening continued and the company seemed to improve and I overrode the very curt remark. After driving me home, we agreed to meet again as soon as our calendar activity allowed.

Thus, began a wonderful journey together based on deep love and most of all friendship and respect, with an acceptance of each other for who we need to be and without major demands on each other's time.

When it came to light that Sylvia had been a team Country Dancer at School, plus Brian wanted "show me off" to the band, I was invited along one evening. I had to wear black trousers and a red blouse or shirt which I luckily already possessed. Just needed to invest in a suitable pair of feminine boots or shoes that were elegant but practical. Much to my surprise I was invited up one evening when the guitar player's wife– usual demo girl could not attend- to demonstrate a dance with him. It was great fun to be doing dances and sequences I recalled from my youth. The rest of the band accepted me and eagerly chatted about my experience of being in the school dancing team and winners of a Middlesex Trophy. Sylvia then attended many bookings and became a part of the team, interacting with the organisers and "punters" A free supper went down well too unless it was a ploughman's, almost totally wheat and dairy based with a little side salad of lettuce and tomato plus of course delicious looking Gateaux and fruit pie for dessert. On these evenings I took my "healthy" alternative and drooled over desserts in particular – always had a sweet tooth and was a quite a sugar addict until re-programmed via my Nutritionalist! If it was a company function we would sometimes be given a free promotional gift. I still have a delightful brightly coloured nylon sports bag I received one evening.

As Demo girl I would partner Brian and join in with some of the dances. This was more challenging, especially in dances which were progressive and couples changed partners throughout the dance routine or we joined a "square set" or "longways set" dance. "Oh! Here we are with the experts" they would laughingly cry "Best get it right!" Then there were

Yes – I Found My Soulmate!!

the times during "progressive" dances when the gentleman would say with great confidence in Sylvia's ability "Oh, I'll be fine now I'm doing it with the expert!" No pressure Sylvia!!! If a slight error occurred we would laugh and they immediately felt more at ease. "If the experts get it wrong, we're OK then!" I miss those times now still – more about that coming up.

Time passed and I had been introduced and accepted by Brian's family and fairly regular visits took place with Christmas stopovers as well. I watched grandchildren grow up and was generally well respected by all family members. Sylvia was at one Christmas event and affectionately called "Nanna Sylvia" by one of his sons then wife. My own family took an immediate liking to my now serious partner and grew to love him. My nieces said he was the Uncle they wished they had had! We have had and still do enjoy great times with them and have also enjoyed their children growing up – two of them now adult and two not far off!!

As the years rolled on we spent a lot of time together, enjoying varied activities and really closely bonding a very strong relationship. Our Spiritual work grew and we supported each other at church services and often worked at events such as Psychic Suppers and Holistic Fairs together. As Sylvia's Holistic and Spiritual career developed with Spiritual development groups and local workshops becoming commonplace activities, the back-up and practical support continued. There has been nothing more joyous for Sylvia than to have someone you love deeply, sharing the same basic spiritual philosophy together. Something she has always both valued and desired.

Brian worked for many years in the kitchen sales industry and was very successful. Both being busy people, we arranged quality time between both our properties, plus holiday breaks and life had a "routine" of sorts. We were the happy couple that my niece's children always believed were married.

All was well until Sylvia began to notice things with her lovely man that caused concern and showed signs of what she had been involved with during her Nursing Home days – Pre Alzheimers Disease symptoms. What do I do? He is still functioning almost normally but doing things totally out of character for a very "organised" gentleman whose car was ritually cleaned every weekend till it shone like a showroom car plus a **very** disciplined routine for things. This was subsequently to turn out to be very useful in respect of memory. It was obvious he was trying to hide things, bless his heart. As I watched, I knew I had to seek advice. We had always talked everything through in our relationship but this was very different as I dreaded having to confront him with his challenges. Once a week when we were not spending time together, I went to the local Altzheimers Society Carers Support evenings to gather information and gain courage to confront him. Eventually I was given a major "nudge" from my Spirit Guide and bit the bullet. Risking an outrage, I asked him to sit down as I had something I had to tell him and proceeded to share my observations plus how I had been "living a lie", to help me be sure of what I had to confront him with. Amazingly, he did accept what I had to say and even admitted some challenges he was experiencing.

The diagnostic journey began and we shared this together, dealing with many appointments and ongoing tests until diagnosis was officially confirmed. Somehow, we dealt as positively as possible with his diagnosis, with Sylvia dealing with her own grieving process – sometimes well and sometimes maybe "not so well" as she did her best to come to terms with all the implications, plus following her Spiritual calling. Many a long night was to become a vital part of this journey, as we shared our feelings and the possible future challenges. These late nights seemed somehow to bind us even more closely together with a realisation dawning, that the love we shared was a mutual expression of God's love through physical form. Knowing that God's Love conquers all, had a major impact on how this journey could be shared together, including Sylvia's other Spiritual purpose activities. Whether or not we should marry, suddenly somehow, became an important factor of our relationship and as Brian so aptly put it, many times, following an eventual proposal, endorsed this, as I share this chapter writing with him - "It seemed the right thing to do as we have been together for all this time, know each other so well, get on together so well, plus, how much we still love each other and all the fun we have had together. I knew that it would happen one day!"

Sylvia loved him from her soul and knew that if he asked her to marry him she would say "yes". During the late night discussions she did tell him this, but did not ever want to do the formal proposing - he had been through a challenging previous marriage and divorce and had built up reluctance to marrying again for many years.

Well what a surprise took place on Valentine's Day of 2013!!

Yes – I Found My Soulmate!!

Brian now was not working and most mornings would walk to a local Coffee & Snacks "club" run by our Local Authority where the "Over Fifties" meet for gossip and snacks. Local groups also gather here – it is typically popular with a Knit and Natter group of ladies who gather round a table or two clicking there needles whilst having a good old "natter" about things and the charity they are knitting for. I usually met Brian around lunch time, whereby we went back to his house for lunch together. On this memorable day, I was running a little late as I had been to a Networking function with my Holistic Coach/Healer hat on during that morning.

When I entered the building and said hello to all (about ten or so present on that day), a head turned round and the whole body rose to its feet turning with it as the voice uttered "Your late aren't you? Never mind I'll forgive you as you're going to marry me anyway aren't you?" For once in her now more vocal years, Sylvia was actually speechless with shock!! The thought of him actually independently proposing like this was the last thing to be expected. As I stood frozen to the spot in what seemed like quite a time frame, a voice was heard to say from one of the ladies "Well you are going to yes aren't you?" The reality of the proposal now set in and Sylvia responded with" Of course I am" as she walked over to hug and kiss her man. Applause filled the room, as the Manager came out of her office to congratulate the "Very Happy Couple". Over a romantic meal out that same evening, we discussed buying an engagement ring and Sylvia who always liked to be somewhat frugal herself, said she would be happy to be given a second hand ring. Saturday was spent browsing and the mission accomplished with a "bargain" of a beautiful pink sapphire ring followed by lunch and plans for the great day.

We decided on my mother's birth date and excitement and happiness was flowing between us. However due to a "surprise sudden announcement", the wedding had to be temporarily put on hold until further tests, undergone by Brian took place before the wedding could go ahead. A few traumas and dramas took place until – "Yes, you can now get married" is heard down the telephone early one morning. Positive shock and typically Cancerian, Sylvia cries tears of joy as she hugs her lovely man! Hurried arrangements, and we are married the following week! In spite of our challenges with the Alzheimers journey we are constantly researching natural ways to hold back or reverse the symptoms plus we communicate honestly about our feelings, live as normal AND LAUGH EVERY DAY!!

Somehow life seems more balanced with a husband who appreciates everything, Spiritual Life Purpose running alongside and doors opening for success! You see, it is great to create our visions and hold our dreams close to our heart and believe in them **BUT** we must allow the Divine timing to come in and show the way to achieve our dreams that benefits our overall earthly life balance and Soul Purpose. This means that they can be achieved in ways to benefit us on our soul journey and are somewhat different to how we may have, through the Ego (edging God out), perceived them to happen. It is amazing how determination along with flexibility best serves our purpose!

A successful Partnership/Marriage is based on:-

- Mutual unconditional love that doesn't judge but is accepting of who each other is and needs to be
- Friendship
- Trust
- Honesty
- Communication – talk everything through instead of having a head to head "I must win" argument
- Forgiveness
- Respecting each other values
- It's OK to see things differently. It is Insecurity that needs both parties to "think the same" about everything
- Seeing humour in tragic situations

SO finally..........

Chapter 8

Creating Balance is The Key

Sylvia's life journey has to date been one of a journey that began as "The Skinned Rabbit" to on-going rebalancing. Through the ups and downs of all the experiences, she can now see as beautiful learning experiences as she remembers who she truly is – a part of the great creative source expressing through a physical body temple.

To be able to view life as experience and be the observer of life, facilitates a wonderful connection to who we truly are and then the key to balancing life is to follow the inner guidance. Daily "silence" or as Dr Wayne Dyer says – contemplation is essential to a fulfilled life that is lived "on purpose".

How do I achieve silent times, you may be thinking? Especially if your life is hectic and your home is full of noisy occupants. Why not take a walk in nature or even a walk in your garden and connect with nature for a few minutes each day? Maybe you have to discipline yourself to get up earlier in the morning to have your "Stillness" time. There is a little phrase in the Bible that says "Be Still and know that I am God" If we are part of God and that is within us, doesn't it make sense to communicate regularly? Would it not seem essential to go within and feel the joy, the love, the peace that is the real you? Then bring that through into your daily experience and see how you begin to become the observer of situations rather than "in the thick of it" and seemingly having no solutions to challenges. The answers to this physical life journey lie deep within, in that part of you that lives on, when we step out of the physical body shell. This is the real you that chose to come here to the earth and knows how to create a world that serves you. The real you that CAN and WILL guide you through difficult times. If you need help with something in life and know the person who could give that help, doesn't it make sense to communicate with them? If you needed a carpenter or plumber to fix something for you, how are they going to know that unless you speak with them and tell them what the problem is. Just the same – if we seek guidance and answers on decisions and our life purpose, then the best person to communicate with, is the "I AM" or God presence within us. In that stillness one can ask for help and receive answers. The answer may come as an inner voice or an inner knowing. Sometimes the answer will manifest through another person who shows up at the right time, through a few words on a bill board in the street – even the words of a song. There are answers and signs all around us and within us. Our part is to be open to recognising them and then act on the guidance.

This truly is the key to a more balanced life.

Let's imagine a life experience divided into segments and in the centre is the Soul, the "I AM" part of us.

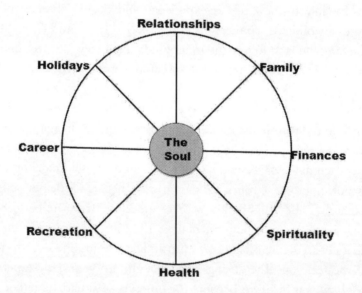

As you contemplate each area of your life you may find that some areas score well and others are not working well for you. By going deep within, beyond the clutter of the mind which has become filled with programming from the influence of others and external environments a connection is begun to that soul part of you. Follow that guidance and draw the creative energy from there, then bring that through into daily life experiences for a greater balance.

This does take discipline and regular practice plus an honest observation of how life is serving you initially. Then allow the inner guide to reveal what you truly desire to be and do here on the earthly journey.

Once revealed, then let the burning desire to achieve, fill your whole being and start writing down your desires and goals for the key areas of your life. Let go any "I can't" or "Should I really?" "What will THEY say?" and just allow your childlike spirit to dance in the joy of creation.

The next step is to write these goals down with dates by them:

- Which you will achieve and when
- Create a visual board or scrap book which you look at daily
- Go within every morning and before you go to bed and feel the experience of having achieved your goals
- Take action on the inner guidance that comes to you
- Believe in those goals and expect good for yourself
- Allow Divine Timing and be Flexible with how they are achieved, whilst remaining focused.
- Live as if they were happening NOW!

It is important to accept that there will be challenges as you create your new life. But as you go within on a daily basis and live each moment to its fullest, patience and persistence can be acknowledged and applied.

Remember: Most of all, ENJOY life and keep things simple.

- Know that life is a journey of experiences, allow them to serve you well and see the lessons within them.
- Let go of the past and live in the present moment at all times.
- Plan your future but enjoy each moment along the way.

As it says in the Tao:
"The journey of a thousand miles begins with one small step!"

Enjoy each step!!

Sylvia's journey from a "Skinned Rabbit" to living her Life Purpose has been truly awesome when reflected on. It is a joy to serve humanity from my learning.

May Your on-going life's journey be in accordance with your soul's purpose here on earth.

Life is a Journey of Experiences that will teach powerful things if we will allow it. Enjoy your journey and fully experience all that life offers you.

Be empowered through these experiences and then go and teach others how they can empower their lives.

GO OUT INTO THE WORLD AND CREATE YOUR WORLD. FEAR NOT THE PAST. IT IS BUT A BAG OF EXPERIENCES THAT YOU CHOSE TO ENRICH YOUR SOUL'S EXPERIENCE.

My Blessing to you!
Sylvia

HOW TO CONTACT SYLVIA

Look at her website www.transormationyourgift.com :-

Subscribe to receive your Free Gift and attend Seminars and Live Broadcasts. You will also receive Sylvia's Motivational Videos and Inspiring Blogs and eBooks.

Be alerted to future publications and reserve your own copy – www.transformationyourgift.com/contactsylvia.html